BIRDS FOR REAL

by

Rich Stallcup

Art Credits:

The cover finches, White-throated Swifts, Lucifer Hummingbird, Western Flycatcher, titmice and Sprague's Pipits were drawn by Keith Hansen.

The Sulphur-bellied Flycatcher, American Dipper and Bobolink are by Tim Manolis.

Rich Stallcup is responsible for the swan (which may look more like a boobie) and the generic epidonax.

Library of Congress Catalog Card No.: 85-090384
ISBN: 0-9615073-0-6

Rich Stallcup
P.O. Box 36
Inverness, CA 94937

Dedication

May California Condors
and the spirit of Billy Clow
forever fly freely.

Acknowledgements

No one or two or ten people are responsible for the current renaissance in the field identification of birds. There are many.

Some of those indirectly responsible for the notions in this book are: Alan Baldridge, Laurie Binford, Billy Clow, Howard Cogswell, Dave DeSante, Jon Dunn, Dick Erickson, Jules Evens, Davis Finch, David Gaines, Eugene Hunn, Kenn Kaufman, Guy McCaskie, Joe Morlan, Van Remsen, Will Russell and Jon Winter.

Guy McCaskie read portions of the first draft and made many crisp and excellent suggestions. Will Russell and David Wimpfheimer convinced me to temper some coarse statements.

Jon Dunn, Kenn Kaufman, Paul Lehman and Will Russell read the entire manuscript and each made comments which greatly improved it.

Keith Hansen and Tim Manolis made the pictures and the cover drawing is Keith's.

Susan Peaslee typed and retyped and made many editorial recommendations, most of which were incorporated, and Elizabeth Whitney kindly provided access to her word processing machine. Sue Stallcup made the alphabetical index, helped in final proof and has cheerfully agreed to be the book's circulation department and Connie Gottlund did a critical proofreading. Tom Sander was mightily helpful in an early production and Dick Ellington told he how to turn a stack of paper with words on them into a book.

Finally, without the help of Willow Marten Stallcup this project might have been completed six months earlier than it was.

Thanks to all of these friends and, as they always say, any mistakes and liabilities belong to me.

INTRODUCTION

A bewildering assortment of new bird books, including several field guides for North America, has recently appeared. Competition amongst the guides was fierce, and to choose the best one or ones is not easy. There is one thing they all have in common: some degree of thoroughness and excellence was given up in a race for competitive publication dates.

In particular, the quality of the illustrations, which are the most important feature of any field guide, ranges from excellent to poor in each volume. Books which primarily use photographs are seriously limited in the number of diagnostic features they can show. (A skilled artist's brush may illustrate many more in fewer figures.) Books which use a number of different artists suffer from inconsistency due to varying skill, style, and care taken, causing beginners to wonder "which ones are right?" Books that use illustrators who have not seen many of the animals in life and who do many of the paintings from museum study skins often mistake coloration and markings and *always* mistake the living bird's shape, thus misrepresenting its entire energy.

It is curious that with all the talent which American field ornithologists possess, a factual text has not yet collided with a great artist who personally knows the birds *in life.* It seems perhaps that the Pough-Eckelberry series and Roger Tory Peterson's original field guides have come the closest.

The Guide to Field Identification of Birds of North America—a Golden Guide first appeared in 1966. It was authored by Chandler S. Robbins, Bertel Bruun and Herbert S. Zim and illustrated by Arthur Singer, and it was the first *real* competitor to Peterson's field guides. The facing-page text, sonograms, and great geographical coverage made it extremely popular. Problems with the text centered around its brevity, a dearth of western input, and apparent use of some unverified information. The pictures, on the other hand, while colorful and artistic, were (are) often misleading and sometimes simply wrong. They may have been drawn from study skins which, for example, have white cotton for eyes, making eyerings especially difficult to discern. Thus, eyerings are often misrepresented, affecting the whole facial expression.

The expanded, revised edition of 1983 has far superior text (since western counseling was sought and received) and new maps. There are a surprising number of new, additional pictures, but unfortunately most of the original ones remain unchanged.

In this workbook we plan to point out errors and add relevant field identification information to that given in the Golden Guide. Also we will point out numerous portions of text that are wholly new in this edition. Almost all of these are from us, are to the point, and are very useful. **You may wish to write these facts directly into your copy or emphasize phrases with a felt-tipped pen. Make a group project of it with your class or bird club.**

The sole aim of this book is to provide the birder with more accurate and complete information. It is in no way an attempt to discredit any published work, as all field guides are honest efforts. (Perhaps next year we'll tackle the National Geographic guide's problems.) Finally, we have not weighted this booklet with picky details but have only intercepted real points of concern, and some may reflect a *western* bias.

WHAT IS MISSING?

The most noticeable omission from the revised Golden Guide is that although birds' names have been updated, the sequence in which they appear remains the same. New names are no doubt the most widely known changes in the *American Ornithologists' Union Checklist for Birds of North America*—Sixth Edition, but family revisions and placement of names on the list are those things which are ornithologically important! This guide now differs significantly from the AOU checklist in the order that the birds appear and will continue to differ from all future lists, from the most comprehensive to the simplest. (The Audubon Society Master Guide and the National Geographic Guide have used nearly the proper order.) Since the Golden Guide claims to be a field guide to the birds of North America and, it is hoped, an accurate one, it would have seemed worthwhile to rearrange a few plates and shuffle a few pages for the proper sequence.

Also missing, as in the earlier edition, are pictures and descriptions of juvenile shorebirds in juvenal plumage (note these spellings). That plumage is so different in many cases from "summer" and "winter" that the young birds can look like entirely different species. It *is* the plumage that many people see most, because there *are* so many juveniles in autumn, often with migration routes and timing quite different than those of adults. Much moaning has been heard from birders in recent years about the lack of juvenal plumaged waders pictured in field guides. Two of the new guides now have them. This one does not. It would have been much more helpful to the great majority of people who will use this book to include pictures of these plumages rather than ones of species which have strayed across our borders from all directions.

INCLUSIONS

The inclusion of color pictures of species recorded a handful of times in the outer Aleutians, the Florida Keys, or

Newfoundland are perhaps impressive, but pictures of more plumages of birds familiar to more people (like juvenile waders–and there are many others) would seem more in keeping with the purpose of a field guide for the North American region. They would substantially improve the volume under discussion.

We will not question in detail the species which were and were not included. Consider, however, the presence of two large pictures of Eurasian Blackbird, a species with near zero chance of getting to North America on its own, and the exclusion of Berylline Hummingbird, a species which is practically regular in late summer in southeast Arizona and which has nested in the United States more than once. Or consider the inclusion of two images of Marsh Sandpiper, which has occurred only once in the outer Aleutians (and was not on anyone's list of expected species to show up there!), and the absence of any visual image of Hook-billed Kite, an infamous resident of the lower Rio Grande Valley of Texas which breeds there every year. You will no doubt wonder about other choices of inclusion and exclusion.

VOICE

For most people sonograms are indecipherable, and English language attempts at translating bird sounds are the only things that work for memory. Many new voice descriptions appear in the new text. They are mostly from us, are very helpful, and will be pointed out in this booklet. Many others are offered here. Several rather comical and nearly useless voice interpretations from the previous edition which have been removed and replaced are cryptically pointed out for your entertainment.

MAPS

The range maps have been much improved. In species which occur in but a small part of North America, only that portion of the region is mapped. This permits presentation of much more accurate distributional information. (See the map for Limpkin in the old and new editions.) These maps are far superior to those in the National Geographic Guide which does not even attempt to show migration routes.

Unfortunately, we still detect a lack of accurate treatment for the west. Not only are some presences ignored (Black-bellied Whistling Duck occurs very regularly year-round and breeds successfully in southeast Arizona); some established *trends* are not even mentioned. For example, it is hard to disregard over 100 Blackpoll Warbler records on the California coast each autumn, with a total number of records there in the last score of years of over 1800.

Twenty-nine species of "eastern warblers" have been found in California, and nineteen of these are regular, with several records each year (and a similar occurrence in Arizona, Colorado and other states). On some of the maps for these species there are a couple of faint red stripes near the west coast, but on others there is nothing at all. So the presence of these marks does *not* reflect occurrence status meaningfully. That is, by looking at the maps we find that Bay-breasted and Magnolia Warblers and Ovenbird (even in the Sierra!) are migrants along the west coast, but that Blackpoll and Tennessee Warblers and American Redstart, are not included there—there are no red stripes. In fact, the latter three are vastly more common on the west coast than are the former three species. This information could have been corrected with some very simple inquiries.

For other species, like Black-throated Blue Warbler with over twenty records for California per fall, the western half of the continent isn't even on the map! Suggesting that Scarlet Tanager is a regular migrant through California but that Bobolink is not is very strange. These kinds of oversights occur for many other migratory birds in many other families and for many states and provinces other than California. In short, we will have many comments to add to the statement on page 270 that eastern species of wood warblers occur along the west coast—though true, a somewhat inadequate remark.

Also, the Golden Guide includes Mexico for ranges of North American birds. There are innumerable mistakes here, many of which are the same mistakes made by authors of Mexican bird guides. Since, however, there is an attempt, we here correct some of the errors known to us, especially for **west mainland Mexico and Baja.** There are doubtless as many mistakes for central and eastern Mexico.

NEW TEXT

Very few people actually sit down and read the text of a field guide. Anyone who has been birding for a long time, though, has had occasion to read most of it in small parts over the years.

There are considerable new pieces of text in the revised edition, most of which came from the west and some of which has become common knowledge. We will point out new passages that we think are valuable. You may wish to highlight them in your copy of the book with pink or yellow marking pens (dark ones show through to the other side of the page).

A final word to the reader about to make use of this workbook: it is necessary to refer directly to the appropriate page in the revised edition for any of the following to make sense.

WE

Most of the thoughts that follow are results of field observation of birds by a number of people, many of whom are listed under acknowledgements. Because it is mostly consensus, I have often chosen to use pronouns such as 'we' and 'us' rather than 'I' and 'me.'

THE STUFF

YELLOW-BILLED LOON – On page 19 the picture of the winter bird is too dark with the bill much too clearly bright yellow. **In Life** these birds have a fuzzy definition between the brown crown and nape and the white cheek. The brown is paler and frosted with light gray. The bills of basic plumaged birds, though invariably having a *pale culmen* are often quite dusky—especially at the base. A very good mark vaguely alluded to in the text but not shown on the illustration is a post-ocular spot of brown which juts forward from the nape into the white cheek behind the eye. See Common Loon bill shape below. Summer (alternate) YBL has purple, not green iridescence.
Text: The fourth sentence is new and valid. Add the fact that the species occurs solitarily or in pairs and usually flies 50–100 meters above the surface.
Map: The species winters regularly in tiny numbers as far south as Monterey, California.

COMMON LOON – On page 19 the picture of the winter bird is too pale. **In Life** the birds are darkest chocolate to nearly black. Although the definition of dark upperparts and white underparts is truly fuzzy, there is always one or more clear white peninsulas that invade the dark of the lower neck. Birds in any plumage of this species and of Yellow-billed Loon have large rectangular heads often with a distinct,

rounded bump on the forecrown. The bills of Commons always have a *dark culmen* but are often light (light blue to creamy) laterally and not always evenly tapered. On some birds the angle on the gonys (profile edge of lower mandible) is nearly as sharp as that of a smiley Yellow-billed loon, and some young Yellow-billeds have a nearly straight gonys.
Text: Add usually solitary or in pairs and flies often 50–100 meters above the surface.

ARCTIC LOON – On page 19 the "winter" bird should have sharper definition between white underparts and dark upperparts; the eye should be more clearly in the black; the nape and hindneck should be frosty gray contrasting the otherwise black dorsal neck; and the bill should be black. The head shape of all these Arctics should be less long with more rounded forecrowns and sloped hindcrowns. The two alternate plumaged birds here show Red-throated Loon-like head shapes. **In Life** winter adults have blackish backs, some with small, jelly-bean-shaped white spots towards the rear of the scapulars; chinstraps which vary from moderate to very obvious (these dark chinstraps give Arctics a unique, white-throated look); sharp vertical stripes on the sides of the neck near the waterline; and faint white spots on some wing coverts. First-winter birds have dark gray backs with slim whitish edges to many of the feathers (especially scapulars); chinstraps which are weak or nonexistent; dull vertical stripes on the sides of the neck near the waterline; and they lack any spotting on the wing coverts.
Text: Add: this species is highly gregarious in its normal range, often in flocks. Usually flies low, just above the waves, although some flocks of spring migrants will be high. While on the water, usually in flocks in deeper, offshore zones. Migrants often rest briefly in sheltered bays.

RED-THROATED LOON – On page 19 the neck of the basic plumaged RTL is too dusky on the sides and the eye is trespassing too far into the gray. These birds are really white-

necked and faced. The head shape is unique. A sloped forecrown and domed hindcrown gives the whole front end an upturned look which is responsible for the upturned flight profile. In Arctic the domed forecrown and sloped hindcrown as well as its black, slightly downcurved bill gives a drooped look to the front end in flight.
Text: Sometimes migrates in loose, disconnected flocks but never as social as Arctic. While on the water, usually solitary and nearshore in bays, harbors and just behind the breakers.

WESTERN GREBE – On page 21 note that there are two easily identified forms which may be good species. The one pictured is *A. o. occidentalis* which has (as shown) a greenish yellow bill with dark ridges and dusky tip; the eye in the dark part of the face; dark sides and a doubled vocalization, a croaked "arrah arrah." *A. o. clarkii* has a large, all yellow-orange bill; the eye is in the light part of the face; the sides are whiter, higher on the bird; and the vocalization is a single croaked "arrah" (rising). This single note is longer than either single element of *occidentalis'* call.

RED-NECKED GREBE – On page 21 the basic plumaged bird's cheek is much too white for most individuals. **In Life** the entire face is usually dirty with a crescent of white at the posterior side. Both birds pictured are more erect-necked than ones away from breeding areas really are. Red-neckeds are regularly scrunched down like Horned Grebes, not stretched up like Westerns.
Text: It should be mentioned that the white patageal feathers (leading edge of the inner wing) are very contrasty white on black and look like headlights if the bird is flying at you.

HORNED GREBE – On page 21 the basic plumaged bird should not have a crest at the hindcrown. **In Life** the crown is flat to rounded. The bird's back slopes into the water.
Text: The last sentence is new and most helpful.

EARED GREBE – On page 21 the basic plumaged bird is not cresty enough, is too dark on the neck and face for most individuals and has too low a rump for most. **In Life** there is a pointy crest on top of the head. Many individuals are very white-necked and cheeked leaving shape more useful for I.D. than pattern. Eared's bill is thinner and appears slightly upturned, its neck is relatively thin, it is usually crested, and the butt is fluffed and held high.
Text: The last six words of the first sentence are new and helpful.

PIED-BILLED GREBE – On pages 20–21 there is no mention of the distinct first winter plumage. Those birds' bodies are a darker, richer brown than adults', the neck and face are orangy brown, and the bill is orangy yellow. There is no eye-ring, black throat or other facial markings. This uniform plumage is, no doubt, that which is mistaken for Least Grebe at times.

LAYSAN ALBATROSS – On page 23 the underwing pattern is too crisp for most Laysans. **In Life** the whole underwing has more extensive dark borders, and the black-white definition is more blurred.
Text: Since several other species of white albatross might be seen in North American waters it might be of value to know basically what things to look at for later reference identification. In descending order of usefulness, note underwing pattern (sharp or blurred, leading and trailing edge), bill pattern and color, head color (dark feathers near eye?), and back color.
Text: Maybe they seldom follow large ships, but birders on fishing boats can usually chum them in.

BLACK-FOOTED ALBATROSS – On page 23 it should be shown that old, worn birds can be very creamy white on most of the underparts, the face and wing coverts. It is not an uncommon condition and those birds need close scrutiny. Black-footed x Laysan hybrids are known.

NORTHERN FULMAR – On page 25 more plumages should be shown. As it is, the white below, gray above bird is the almost exclusive plumage of Atlantic birds. The gray one shown is that which in normal years is at a ratio of 9:1 over light phases off the west coast in winter. There are, however, other plumages which *at least* need a mention. Double dark and double light are virtually black and white respectively. Mottled ones can have different combinations of dark and light and resemble other species like Cape Petrel. The gray bird shown should have white-shafted primaries.
Text: It should be mentioned that fulmars have very round heads accentuated by their chunky, yellow bills. The wingtips are also more rounded than those of shearwaters.

CORY'S SHEARWATER – On page 25 note that Cory's often have white upper tail coverts very similar to those of Greater Shearwater.

PINK-FOOTED SHEARWATER – On page 25 the underwing pattern is wrong. **In Life** the underwing is variously dusky but always with an unmarked white core, and leading and trailing edges are the darkest feathers on the bird. The underwing coverts are not piano keyboard as shown. The bills of all individuals are bright pink with the distal one-third sharply black. The legs and feet, although visible as the bird runs on the water to gain flight, are buried in feathers during flight. The bird is, for field purposes, exactly like Cory's in size and shape. It is not noticeably smaller with radically deeper, raked wings as shown.

SOOTY SHEARWATER – See Short-tailed Shearwater below. On page 27 the underwing pattern is wrong for all individuals. **In Life** the lesser underwing coverts and remiges (flight feathers) are usually black while the median and greater underwing coverts are silvery white.

SHORT-TAILED SHEARWATER – This bird from Sooty Shearwater ranks with such things as Plegadis Ibises and silent meadowlarks in the top ten most difficult identification problems in North America. No one character will identify it. On page 27 the underwings are too dark, the bill is too long, the forecrown is too sloped and the head is too uniformly dark for the species. **In Life** the underwing pattern, often uniform smoky white, is generally what is shown on page 27 for *Sooty Shearwater* while Sooties in fresh plumage show silvery white linings (coverts for the underside of flight feathers) but dark remiges (the actual stiff flying feathers). The bill is shorter than Sooty's, dramatically so in some individuals. The forecrown is very steep from the base of the culmen giving this species a more rounded head than Sooty Shearwater. Many Short-taileds are subtly dark-capped and light-throated.

FLESH-FOOTED SHEARWATER – On page 27 the bill is too dark and the feet are visible. **In Life** the bill is sharply bright pink or whitish pink in the basal two-thirds and black on the distal one-third. In normal flight the legs and feet are entirely covered by belly and crissal feathers.

BULLER'S SHEARWATER – On page 27 the shape is not right and the ventral and dorsal wing patterns are misleading. **In Life** the birds appear very long-winged and the wings are smoothly bowed not raked (bent at the wrist). The underwing is immaculate with sharp, conspicuous, black emarginations on the leading and trailing edges. The leading and trailing edges of the dorsal surface inside the wrist are whiter than shown, thus emphasizing the gray back, black cap, primaries and carpal bar. There is no duskiness in the face as shown.

Text: Add that sometimes homogenous flocks are seen and their synchronized flight is beautifully graceful.

AUDUBON'S SHEARWATER – Should show more extensive dark feathering below the belly.

MANX SHEARWATER – Underside of remiges should be less black and more silver.

BLACK STORM-PETREL – The forked tail is rarely seen (see new text).
Text: The second-to-the-last sentence is new.

ASHY STORM-PETREL – On page 31 both birds are too black and show too much of a forked tail. **In Life** Ashy is brown–much more so than Black and Least–and the greater secondary coverts above are tan. Worn birds are quite pale and care must be taken not to call them Fork-taileds, especially when there is back lighting. Because of shallow wing strokes (see new text) the underwing is seldom seen. Ashies are springtailed and the tail is long.
Text: The last six words are new and valid. Add that although wing elevation will identify Blacks from Ashies in normal flight, both take high strokes while accelerating to gain flight.

FORK-TAILED STORM-PETREL – On page 31 the picture is better than in the old edition as they have added a wash of gray to the underparts. It is still too bicolored. **In Life** Fork-taileds are practically uniform pearl gray above and below with black auriculars or ear coverts (the patch of feathers behind the eye), black underwing coverts, and dark carpal bars (diagonal across the upper wing surfaces from the body to the wrists). The flight feathers are not dark as shown. The bird has a larger, rounder head.
Map: Fork-taileds are rarely encountered at sea in recent years south of Oregon.

LEACH'S STORM-PETREL – On page 31 the Leach's is much too black with too much white at the base of the tail for birds in the Northeast Pacific (possibly OK for sub-arctic

populations). **In Life** our birds are dark brown, intermediate in color between Black and Ashy. Off Northwest Mexico there are Leach's with entirely dark rumps, and this form has occurred in Southern California. Even the lightest-rumped ones off British Columbia, Alaska and the North Atlantic have a dark smudge up the middle of the white.
Text: Add that off the west coast they are seldom seen within thirty miles of shore.

WILSON'S STORM-PETREL – **Map**: A small oversight: Wilson's is regular in tiny numbers off of California nearshore. **Text**: Although the webbing between the black toes is yellow, it is difficult to see and would not be one of the first things to look for.

LEAST STORM-PETREL – **Text**: In the second sentence the fourth word and the last six words are new and important. Add that they are the most bat-like of all the North Pacific Storm-Petrels because of their high wing strokes and tailless look.

BAND-RUMPED STORM-PETREL – **In Life** the rump is more extensively white than shown and lacks the dividing stripe of Leach's (see above).

WEDGE-RUMPED STORM-PETREL – Occurs irregularly off California and should be mentioned on page 30 and/or shown on page 31. It is small and dark like a Least with similar high, rapid wingbeats but it looks long-tailed. The upper tail coverts are white and extremely long, covering much of the actual tail but tapering towards the tip. Unlike Wilson's the white is not obvious when the bird is perched on the water. The reason for this is that the white is confined to the rump area and does not extend to the sides of the flanks or vent area. The long white rump feathers above the tail are covered by the closed wings.

WHITE-TAILED TROPICBIRD – **Text**: Add that Atlantic adults have yellow to deep orange (not red) bills, and those of Pacific birds are decidedly greenish.
Map: The species also occurs in the Pacific and has reached California and Arizona.

MAGNIFICENT FRIGATEBIRD – **Map**: Delete the blue dotted line off California north of Southern Baja.

RED-FOOTED BOOBY – On page 35 the immature, the age which usually occurs in the continental U.S., is missing. **In Life** immatures are tan, have bubble-gum pink (thanks, Davis) bill bases and dull pink legs and feet.

BROWN BOOBY – **Text**: Add that adult males of west coast *S. l. brewsterii* have frosty gray-white crowns and napes.

BRANDT'S CORMORANT – **Text**: The last sentence is new and valid.

DOUBLE-CRESTED CORMORANT – **Text**: The last sentence is new and valid.

PELAGIC CORMORANT – **Text**: The last sentence is new and valid.

OLIVACEOUS CORMORANT – **Text**: Add that it has a very long, wedge-shaped tail and holds its neck crooked in flight (like Double-crested) giving a unique shape. That part of the bird behind the trailing edge of the wing can appear even longer than that part before the leading edge.

RED-FACED CORMORANT – **Text**: Add that adults have brown wings that contrast their iridescent black bodies and have white flanks in summer. Adults and immatures have pale, blue or horn-colored bills (Pelagics always have black).

TUNDRA SWAN – On page 41 the case is too clear cut. **In Life** Whistling type Tundra Swans sometimes lack the yellow spot and many have a red cutting edge to the bill. The immatures can be difficult to call by bill pattern, and often bill and head *shape* are all that work.

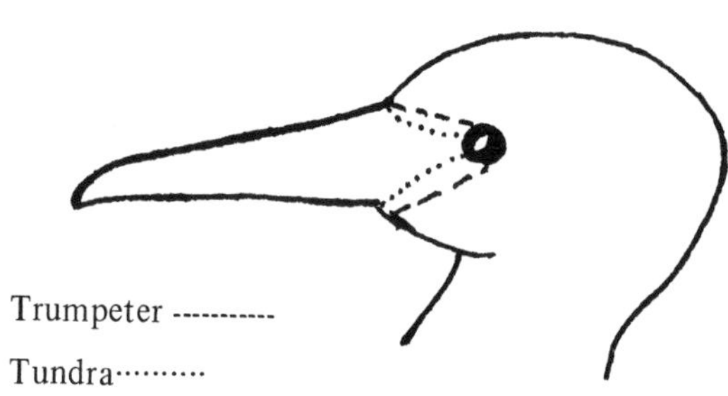

Difference at eye: wider angle for Trumpeter

SNOW GOOSE – **Text:** In the last sentence the fourth and fifth double-words are new and valid.

ROSS' GOOSE – On page 45 the immature Ross' Goose is still too dark and has the wrong bill color. The adult's head is too flat and its bill is too big. **In Life** basic plumaged immature Ross' Geese are even whiter and have pink not black bills. Agency censuses from aircraft sometimes identify homogenous flocks of Ross' by their uniform whiteness. Immature Snow Geese are quite gray. The Ross' Goose has a very round head and very short bill.
Text: The last two sentences are new and significant.

CINNAMON TEAL – On page 51 the sitting female is too pale with too few scalloped markings and the face is too plain. **In Life** the birds are usually richer, darker brown, and have mottled flanks and sides.

Text: It is difficult to understand the meaning of the last four words in the second-to-the-last sentence for two reasons: the illustrations on page 51 do not show this; and it is not obvious in living birds. Female Cinnamons have less distinct facial markings than female Blue-wingeds (whose facial pattern more resembles female Green-winged Teal's). Since the previous edition did not try to separate female Cinnamon and Blue-winged Teal, the *beginning* of the third sentence is new and valid.

WOOD DUCK – On page 53 my copy shows a green neck and underwing for the lower right-hand flying bird. Obviously this is not true in life, and is most likely a printing slip, not an error.

BLACK-BELLIED WHISTLING DUCK – **Map:** On page 52 the species occurs year-round in small number in southeast Arizona, and is common there in summer. It nests there!

TUFTED DUCK – **Text:** On page 54 (under Ring-necked Duck) the last line is misleading. **In Life** many females have white crescents or partial crescents on the face, laterally at the base of the bill.

GREATER SCAUP – **Text:** On page 54 add that Greater's bill is relatively larger than Lesser's, is more spatulate and the nail is larger (all pictured). On some males, not only the nail but the entire bill tip is black. In summer, most females have a tan dime-sized post-ocular spot which contrasts with the darker brown head. A trace of it may be seen on some Lesser Scaup in summer. In mid-winter, few birds of either species show it.

LESSER SCAUP – **Text:** On page 54 add that Lesser's head is not evenly arched as is Greater's but is more squared, often with a distinct angle at the nape, often with some loose, unruly feathers there. The male shown on page 55 is quite good on head shape.

BARROW'S GOLDENEYE – On page 57 the pictures of the females are misleading. Common is shown with large white areas at the closed wing and Barrow's is all gray. **In Life** there is no such difference and the presence or lack of white there depends upon feather arrangement.
Text: Currently there seems to be continent-wide confusion as to bill color in females of this species, and possibly it stems from geographic variation. It should be mentioned that while the bill of non-adult males in the east is usually yellow, it is often blackish (darkest green, darkest orange) in the west. These brighten up in the spring. In the west, some hatching-year males and possibly *some* adult females have entirely yellow, orange or pink bills. The bill of Barrow's is seldom bicolored (except nail), and that of Common often is. The nail at the tip of Barrow's bill is dark, even when the rest of the bill is colored. The nail of female Common's bill is often orange like the bill tip.

COMMON GOLDENEYE – See Barrow's Goldeneye above.
Text: It is noteworthy that while the bill of many female plumaged birds is all jet black, many others are black with an orange tip or orange with a black base.

OLDSQUAW – **Text:** On page 60 it should be mentioned that most individuals at the south end of the winter range are immatures lacking the long tail feathers of adult males and many having scruffy plumage. Males in any plumage may be told by the subterminal band of pink on the bill.

BLACK SCOTER – On page 60 the underwings of the flying birds are wrong. As the *new* text in the second-to-the-last sentence suggests, the underwings are frosty and grayish, visible at a great distance.

WHITE-WINGED SCOTER – **Text:** On page 60 add that the white spots on the immature female's head are variable in size and shape, that the dorsal ridge of the bill is slightly concave, and that the feathering extends to the nostril unlike other scoters. Also add that males in molt become very strange, with patchy tan and white and have been mistaken for eiders.

SURF SCOTER – **Text:** On page 60 add that the white spots on the female's head are variable in size and shape and that the dorsal ridge of the bill is slightly convex. Most birds in female plumage are black-capped while White-wingeds are not. In reference to the last line of text, Surfs along the west coast, at least, usually fly in lines.

HOODED MERGANSER – On page 63 the side of the male in my copy are too dull for most birds. **In Life** the sides are more cinnamon.

RED-BREASTED MERGANSER – On page 63 the head is too dark on the female, and none of the bills are red enough. **In Life** females have light rusty heads, and all Red-breasted and Commons have bright red bills.
Text: Add that birds in ratted plumage may be told from Commons by bill characteristics. In both sexes the nostril is farther out the bill and the facial feathering extends onto the bill in the nasal groove. Compared to Common Merganser's bill, Red-breasted's is thicker throughout. Common's bill is very deep at the base, and the taper towards the tip is extreme.

COMMON MERGANSER – **Text:** Add that birds in molt or badly worn individuals may be told from Red-breasteds by bill characteristics. In both sexes the nostril is closer to the face and the facial feathering stops sharply at the base of the bill.

MASKED DUCK – **Text:** A behavioral trait is important. Add that birds of this species are reclusive and hide very efficiently in aquatic vegetation.

FEMALE DUCKS IN FLIGHT – On page 64 several birds are out of scale. Most notable is that in reality Wood Ducks are small, barely bigger than Coots, and Fulvous Whistling Ducks are as big as small geese. Page 65 is better, although

Surf and especially White-winged Scoters are distinctly bigger than Blacks. Common Eiders fly with their bills pointed slightly downward, giving them a blunt-headed look, like wildebeests, different from all of the scoters.

BLACK VULTURE – Contrary to what it says in the text on page 66, Black Vultures have quick, twinkly flaps compared to Turkey Vulture. The flaps are not so labored.

CALIFORNIA CONDOR – **Text**: On page 66 the first six words of the second sentence are new and important. Add that while soaring, Condors occasionally "double-dip." This motion is two, quick (for a bird that size–they look to be slow motion), deep flaps preceded and followed by soaring. It is unique to the species.

MISSISSIPPI KITE – **Text**: On page 68 it might be mentioned that one-year-olds have adult body feathering but retain barred juvenal tails and some brown in the wings.
Map: There are scattered breeding colonies as far west as southeastern Arizona (Dudleyville, Pinal County).

NORTHERN GOSHAWK – On page 71 the flying first-winter bird shows cottony-white undertail coverts, two of the birds have straight-across tailbands, one has none at all, and the shape of the wings is too much like Sharp-shinned Hawk. **In Life** the immature should have tan-brown blotched (dark, tear-shaped marks around the feather shaft) undertail coverts. In immatures, it is Cooper's that have big fluffy *white* ones. Also, all four illustrations should show wavy tail bands (Goshawks' are always wavy, Cooper's rarely are, and the vast number of Cooper's' and all Sharp-shinneds' tail bands are straight across). Also the wings of the flying birds should be more pointed, less round. Sharp-shinneds have the shortest, roundest; Cooper's longer, slightly pointier; and Goshawks the longest, pointiest of Accipiters' wings.

COOPER'S HAWK – On page 71 the flying adult is the wrong shape. Also the terminal tailbands of the perched birds are virtually missing and that of the flying juvenile is too dark. The undertail coverts of the immatures are shown as uncontrasty and similar to the belly and breast, and the underwing *coverts* are too tan and too highly patterned. **In Life** the shape shown for the flying juvenile is more correct with its long tail and neck. The adult should be the same shape. Terminal tailbands for all birds should be wide and *white.* The undertail coverts of the immatures should be *white* and obvious, as should the underwing coverts, the latter lightly barred. It is the juvenile Goshawk, not Cooper's, that has tan, streaked undertail coverts, a dull, narrow white terminal tailband, and highly marked underwing coverts!
Text: Words eleven through fifteen in the second sentence are new.

SHARP-SHINNED HAWK – **Text**: The second-to-the-last sentence should point out that in the far *west* Sharp-shinneds and Cooper's are nearly equal in numbers during migration and in the winter, though "Sharpies" always have a slight edge.

NORTHERN HARRIER – **Text**: It should be pointed out (and one of the five illustrations should show) that juveniles of both sexes are brown (like adult females) with orangy underparts, especially the breast and underwing coverts, and they lack the heavy streaking.

ROUGH-LEGGED HAWK – **Text**: On page 73 all four pictures are of juveniles. It seems that *something* should be done for adults, which may be quite different. **In Life** many adults lack solid black belly bands and have varying amounts of black ventral streaking depending upon gender. Most adults also lack the wide, black, sub-terminal tail band and instead have more and narrower ones.

Text: The fourth sentence is new and alludes to the facts described above.

FERRUGINOUS HAWK – On page 73 the wings of the flying birds are much too rounded and the tail from below is too white. Juvenal plumage (that worn by perhaps half the population in autumn and winter) is not shown at all. **In Life** the wings of all age birds are very pointed while soaring. They are shaped more like Swainson's than Red-taileds as shown. The tail of adults often appears pinkish as they soar. Immature plumage lacks orangy leggings, dorsal tail feathers and wing coverts. Instead, the leggings are white (as the rest of the underparts), the tail feathers are white with various amounts of gray blotching subterminally, and the "shoulders" are brown (like the rest of the dorsal wing). Juvenal plumaged birds (in the nest and freshly fledged) are brown-headed and could be passed off as adult Swainsons!!
Text: The one-word second-to-the-last sentence is new, is true, and is completely contradictory to what is said in older editions.

RED-TAILED HAWK – In the west this species is highly variable. There are black ones, brown ones, orangy ones, and cream-colored, brown-hooded ones. Few western individuals have black belly bands.
Text: Words 15, 16, and 17 of the second sentence are misleading for a guide to North American birds because most Red-taileds in the *west lack* such contrast abdominally. Also the first six words of the fourth sentence may be nullified because Ferruginous Hawk is bigger and every bit as heavy. The last two words of sentence six are true but it aches to be said that the species is frequently seen "kiting." That is whiffling the wings at sufficient speed and rhythm to remain stationary while flying into the wind. It very much resembles hovering and serves the same purpose. Under Harlan's Hawk (when it still was considered a species) concerning the "light

phase" my friend Guy McCaskie once tightly summed it up as "an unknown form of a nonexistent species."

SWAINSON'S HAWK – **Text:** Words 3, 4 and 5 of sentence five are new. The wings are pointed. Add the fact that the bird is very *long*-winged, especially obvious from the length of the primaries relative to the length of the tail on perched birds.

BROAD-WINGED HAWK – **Map:** On page 74 note that Broad-wingeds are regular migrants (20 per autumn at Point Diablo) and rare winter visitors in California.

RED-SHOULDERED HAWK – On page 75 the adults are too dull and the immature too pale for western examples (*B. l. elegans*) and the flying birds lack the most glaring wing feature (though it is mentioned in the text). **In Life** western ones are much redder below and have more striking checkerboard wings and wider white and sharper black tailbands. Western immatures are darker than the nominate race and than the one shown. Also the white crescents at the base of the primaries above and below are obvious and unique. Both adults and immatures possess them.
Text: Add to the first sentence that they are also very common along coastal California. At the end add that the voice is a whistled scream with the quality of a Red-tailed Hawk but much shorter and in series about one per second "phew-phew-phew-phew-phew-phew-phew."

HARRIS' HAWK – **Text:** Add that it has been re-introduced into parts of its former range like the Colorado River Valley of California. Also while it is common in Baja Sur it is very rare in Baja Norte west of the watershed.

COMMON BLACK HAWK – **Map:** Also breeds sparsely in west Texas, New Mexico and Utah.

ZONE-TAILED HAWK – On page 77 the adults, especially the perched one, show too many white tail bands. **In Life** crissal feathers cover a couple of the bands, and usually they show only one plus a white terminal band just like Common Black Hawk. Thus they look much the same in that regard. To tell them apart while perched, look at the soft parts: Common Black Hawk has about 30 percent larger bill with a much bigger yellow cere, and its exposed tarsii (yellow legs) are notably longer than those of Zone-tailed.

GRAY HAWK – The identification problem which is not mentioned is juvenile Gray versus juvenile Broad-winged Hawk.
Text: Add that to tell this species in juvenal plumage from the similar Broad-winged Hawk there are four areas of concern. Gray Hawk has a noticeably larger bill, has some blotchy areas or streaks of rust on the back, has narrowly vermiculated drumsticks, and has a white rump. Broad-wingeds have petite bills, dark backs with occasional whitish feathers, and usually inverted chevrons or bold bars on the drumsticks. Add that the voice is like a western Red-shouldered Hawk, in series but only one call per two or three seconds.

BALD EAGLE – On page 78 and 79 intermediate age birds are not shown or really discussed. **In Life** after the first winter and for the next year or two the *body* as well as the underwings become quite white.
Text: Under White-tailed Eagle add that the wings in flight are often notably raked and the bird then is shaped like a huge Osprey. Because White-tailed Eagle has a very pale head it has been confused with Bald Eagle, but the flight silhouette is rather different.

GYRFALCON – **Text:** On page 80 it should be mentioned (it is well illustrated) that the wings are broad and rounded (for a falcon), not unlike those of a Goshawk.

PRAIRIE FALCON – On page 81 flying juvenal plumage is not shown and a very useful character perhaps cannot be shown. **In Life** juveniles' median and greater underwing coverts are blackish as are the axillaries (wingpits) making large but narrow black triangles on the underwing. Also, flying birds often suggest a pink tail which contrasts the otherwise sandy plumage.

APLOMADO FALCON – **Text**: Should say "extirpated from U.S." On page 80 the first word is an understatement, as an authority has pointed out that there have been no sanitary records in Arizona for over forty years. Allegedly the species nested in New Mexico as recently as 1952 and probably some of the many sight records from West Texas are correct, although there are a lot of miles between there and the nearest population in Mexico.

SNOWY EGRET – **Text**: On page 94 the last eight words in the third sentence are new and pertinent. When the birds hatch, however, their legs are all yellow with the front portion darker. This condition holds through the first winter. Also note that while all ages of Snowy Egret have bare, yellow facial skin, immature Little Blue Herons have gray.

REDDISH EGRET – **Text**: On page 97 add that immatures may have all dark bills and lack the shaggy appearance, but all have a clear, pale iris. Also add that the white color phase is unknown in the western U.S. and is rare on the Pacific coast of Southern Mexico.

LITTLE BLUE HERON – Immatures have grayish tips to primaries.

BLACK-CROWNED NIGHT HERON – **Text**: On page 98-99 it should be pointed out that some second autumn and winter birds have gray crowns and backs, are uniform off-white below.

YELLOW-CROWNED NIGHT HERON – On page 99 the immature's bill is too light and the dorsal wing pattern should be shown. *Actually,* the young have all dark bills (while those of BCNH are mostly greenish-yellow from the base) and have a contrasty dark trailing edge to the wing.

LEAST BITTERN – On page 99 only males are shown, and no mention is made of sexual dimorphism. **In Life** females are duller with brown backs and crowns and more streaking on the ventral neck.

WHITE-FACED IBIS – **Map:** On page 100 the summer range in the west is way too extensive in the north and lacking in the south. In reality it is now a very, very sparse breeder in easternmost California. Also the species is a rather common resident in the Cape region of Baja.

WHITE IBIS – There is a large population in west mainland Mexico and a small population in the Cape Region of Baja. These sources are, no doubt, responsible for the irregular appearance of White Ibis in the southwestern U.S.

SORA – On page 105 the immature is too dull for most examples. **In Life** fall juveniles are much more buffy throughout, there is no black on the face and the bill is dull orange-gray. Birds that look like this have been misidentified as Yellow Rails and/or Corn Crakes (see below).

CORN CRAKE – **Text:** On page 104 add that the species' European population has become very low in recent years and it is improbable that the bird will naturally occur in North America again.

YELLOW RAIL – On page 105 the Yellow Rail seems too dull on the face and breast. **In Life** most individuals are *bright* buffy cream and chestnut below but quite dark above as shown.

Map: On page 104 this is very much in error in the same manner that Peterson's Western Guide was before! In fact there are only two winter records in California in the past 75 years. This map shows California as a major wintering area!!

BLACK RAIL – **Text**: On page 104 add at the end that vocalizations include a low, grating but quiet "gurr, grr, grr" and a piercing "pip-pip."

CLAPPER RAIL – On page 107 the standing bird is too gray for western races and most Gulf Coast birds, and distinctions appear too clear-cut in separation from King Rail. **In Life** many Clappers are rusty orange on the neck and breast and have more warm colors on the back. Also Clappers and Kings are so alike (and there are hybrids) that some experts in areas of sympatry identify them by habitat, a risky method. Cheek color and back pattern are the most consistent differences. **Text**: On page 106 add at the end of the text that the call most often heard is a series of loud descending quacks, similar to but bigger than that of Virginia Rail.

BLACK OYSTERCATCHER – **Text**: On page 110 add that the distal one-third of the bill of a hatching-year bird is blackish.

AMERICAN AVOCET – On page 111 the legs are too dull and it should be noted that the standing bird is a male. **In Life** adult birds have bright powder blue legs and feet. Female Avocets have a more radically upswept bill.

NORTHERN LAPWING – On page 111 the immature bird is not shown, and that is the type that shows up in North America. See them in European guides.

LESSER GOLDEN-PLOVER – On page 113 the bulk of the basic plumaged standing bird is too great and the coloration too gray. **In Life** the head and bill proportions are truly more

like those of Mountain Plover and less like those of Black-bellied Plover. Also autumn-winter birds are quite tan on the breast and flanks and more brown on a back with yellow spots. The auriculars (ear coverts) are often distinctly the darkest part of the face.
Text: On page 112 it is of help to add that the Pacific Lesser Golden-Plover (*P. de. fulva*) (the one that breeds widely in western Alaska and the one that winters on lawns in Hawaii) winters sparingly but regularly, often in flocks, in coastal California and probably other Pacific states. It is slightly smaller than the American race (*P. d. dominica*), is yellower on the face, and has brighter yellow spots on the back. These two forms behave as separate species and may soon be "split."

BLACK-BELLIED PLOVER – **Text:** Add at the end that the clear, mournful call could be written as "too-oo-whee?"

PIPING PLOVER – On page 115 the legs are too dull in my copy. **In Life** the legs and feet are usually bright International Orange.

SNOWY PLOVER – **Text:** On page 114 the parenthesis in the second sentence is new and true.

COMMON RINGED PLOVER – On page 115 there is too short a white mark behind the eye. **In Life** the white behind and above the eye is clearly more extensive than that of Semipalmated Plover, though Semi is variable in this feature within its species.
Text: On page 114 (under Semipalmated Plover) the first part of the last sentence is only half true. Actually there is partial webbing between two of the toes. Semipalmated Plover has partial webbing between all three forward toes. Also the call of Ringed may be more appropriately "softer and in more a minor key" than that of Semi.

MARBLED GODWIT – **Text**: On page 116 add to the second sentence that many worn individuals, juveniles and some winter adults, lack barring below and may be quite white. In the worn birds the marbling on the back is often reduced to nil.

BRISTLE-THIGHED CURLEW – **Text**: Add at the end that the call is much like that of Black-bellied Plover (see above) and has humanlike quality.

WHIMBREL – On page 119 the flying bird at the left could also represent the Asian race of Whimbrel (*N. p. variagatus*) which is a regular migrant to western Alaska, though most Asian birds are intermediate between *N. p. hudsonicus* and the nominate race.
Text: In the last sentence the fourth word might be replaced with the words "panic-stricken" and the call might be written as "tse-tse-tse-tse-tse-tse-tse-tse."

MARSH SANDPIPER – On page 120 note that there is only one record in the western Aleutians and the species is not a part of the avifauna in nearby Siberiasia. Also note that the upperparts in the illustrations are far too dark. **In Life** the upperparts of basic plumaged birds are light gray, not dissimilar to the Wilson's Phalarope.

GREATER YELLOWLEGS – On page 121 the bill is too uniformly black and the flying bird is too stocky. **In Life** Greater's bill is usually gray-based and black-tipped. Also the flying bird's proportions should appear longer and more gangly before and behind the wings.
Text: On page 120 the third sentence is misleading. Actually Wilson's Phalarope (which often forages along the shore), Stilt Sandpiper, Upland Sandpiper, and Ruff (which has become a usual feature of North American birdlife), are all tall and yellow-legged (Ruff often has yellow but also other colors). Also add at the end that the panicky flight call may be written as "too-to-to-to-to" very rapid.

The bill of Greater Yellowlegs is *relatively* longer than most of Lesser Yellowlegs. A shaky rule is that Greater's bill is one-and-one-half or more times the length of the head while Lesser's is one to one-and-one-quarter times the head. Also note that Greater Yellowlegs' legs may be orange or even reddish.

LESSER YELLOWLEGS – On page 120 the call might be written "too-lu-lu." It is quiet and underwhelming compared to the voice of Greater (above).

SOLITARY SANDPIPER – On page 120 add that when flushed the birds often rise rapidly to considerable altitude in *towering* flight while calling a quick, shrill "wheet-weet-weet." Less often they just flit-flit around the corner and settle again.

UPLAND SANDPIPER – **Text**: On page 122 add to the fourth sentence that this species also often flies regularly like a Whimbrel.

BUFF-BREASTED SANDPIPER – **Text**: Page 122 should more strongly emphasize that all birds, especially juveniles, are whitish on the belly and lower breast and lack prominent white eyerings. They simply are not bright buff to the crissum, and this error, which has been passed along book to book, has caused confusion.

RUFF – On page 123 the bills of the standing birds seem too long and straight. **In Life** Ruffs have inordinately short bills that drop near the tip.
Text: Add to the thought in the sixth sentence that all age/sex Ruffs may have red, orange, pink, yellow, green, blue, gray or nearly black legs, though orangy and greenish are most common. Add to the text the following valuable hints. All age/sex Ruffs have long, flexible tertial feathers that can be seen moving on the breeze. Also, note behavior-

ally that Ruffs are very aggressive and pugnacious while feeding. Add that Sharp-tailed Sandpiper in juvenal plumage is the primo look-alike species.

WILLET – On page 123 the pictures of the basic plumaged birds are not correct for western Willets and the leg color is not right in my book. **In Life** western Willets are fairly dark gray above and *do not* have a distinct white supercilium (eyebrow). Also the legs should be thicker and bluer. Note: A careful look at Willets in the previous edition reveals the suggestion that this species molts its hind toes in summer! The question is solved with the new plate where both birds are standing tarsus deep in water.

TEREK SANDPIPER – On page 125 the flying bird is too dark and lacks the two most glaring field marks. **In Life** the upperparts are pale gray or pale gray with occasional black feathers not dark brown as in my copy. Also the secondaries are white, forming a big white wedge on the trailing edge of the wing, and the bill is dramatically upturned like a (male) Avocet's.

SPOTTED SANDPIPER – On page 125 my copy shows an orange rump on the larger flying bird, dark brown upperparts on the perched birds, and dull, pink legs and feet. *Actually* there is no orange on the bird (that is a color slip, not an error). All birds have medium brownish gray upperparts, and the legs and feet are usually yellow.

WANDERING TATTLER – On page 125 the flying bird and the winter bird are too dark and the winter bird's legs and feet are too orange. **In Life** basic plumaged tattlers have pale gray upperparts and nearly white underparts, much reducing the prominence of the white eyebrows. The legs are usually pale yellow not orange-yellow.

DOWITCHERS – **Text**: On page 124 add that autumn birds in juvenal plumage (those with creamy or buffy edges to back and wing covert feathers) may be identified by the pattern on the tertial and greater and sometimes median wing covert feathers. This, for the west coast only. In Long-billeds those feather centers are broadly dark with a thin, pale fringe; in Short-billeds they are striped.

SHORT-BILLED DOWITCHER – **Map**: On page 124 add blue paint to the whole west coast of the Baja Peninsula, around the tip, 20 percent up the east coast, and the entire coast of mainland west Mexico. The species is abundant at spots there in winter.

WILSON'S PHALAROPE – **Text**: Add that the species is uncommon only outside its range, that it often forages along the shore, and that it has long, yellow legs. Juveniles have tan and buffy edges to back and wing feathers.

RED PHALAROPE – **Text**: On page 127 the parenthesis in the second sentence is new and also largely applies to autumn adults.

RED-NECKED PHALAROPE – On page 127 the bills are all too needly, and the winter swimmer is too chunky and too dark-backed. **In Life** this species' bill shape is more like that of Red than it is like that of Wilson's (it almost says this in the text), and they are not as chunky and thick-necked as Reds. Also, winter adults have pale gray backs (like Red). Juvenile birds have black backs, crowns and napes and buffy stripes on the back converging towards the rump.

BLACK TURNSTONE – **Text**: On page 128 the second-to-the-last sentence is new. Leg color is sometimes pinkish or even orange.

ROCK SANDPIPER – On page 129 the winter plumaged bird is too highly patterned for the race most often seen in North America in winter. **In Life** they are uniform medium gray above and except for the bill look much like little Surfbirds.
Map: On page 128 my copy has a printing error. There really is no breeding colony for this species 500 miles off the coast of Oregon!

SHARP-TAILED SANDPIPER – On page 131 the standing bird is a new picture and is much better than the old head-only of a spring adult. It should be more orangy breasted.
Text: Much of the text is new, and the streaked crissum is an important character. They are, however, streaks and not chevrons as illustrated in the flying bird.

PECTORAL SANDPIPER – On page 131 the picture is of a spring adult. Juveniles (the ones mostly seen in autumn and virtually the only ones seen in the west) have narrow vertical streaks instead of chevrons as shown, and the edges to the back feathers and wing coverts are brighter. Also they have two converging white or tan stripes on the back (as does the juvenile Sharp-tailed Sandpiper).

CURLEW SANDPIPER – On page 131 there should be a bird in juvenal plumage. Juveniles are brownish above with scaly looking backs and a rich, peachy wash across the breast, much as Baird's Sandpiper.

DUNLIN – On page 131 the winter ones are too gray for North American Dunlins. **In Life** our Dunlins are uniform medium brown above. How they look at any moment, however, depends upon light, angle, cloudiness and substrate.

LEAST SANDPIPER – **Map**: On page 132 it is inconsistent to show the bird for most of North America and exclude Baja where they are common in appropriate habitat at appropriate seasons.

GREAT KNOT – On page 135 the tail is too dark. **In Life** the tail looks gray, deemphasizing the white rump.

TEMMINCK'S STINT – **Text:** On page 134 add that the legs may also be yellowish brown. The primary call is a shrill rattle and sounds like a distant Black Turnstone.

WINTER PLUMAGE OF SMALLER SHOREBIRDS – On page 136 both the Red Knot and Rock Sandpiper should have nearly uniform gray upperparts and much unpatterned white underparts. The Least Sandpiper should have a brown wash completely across the breast and yellow legs. The Red Phalarope should have dark legs and feet.

JAEGERS – It is a pity that only one non-adult jaeger is shown, and that one does not look wholly like a Parasitic.

PARASITIC JAEGER – **Text:** On page 138 it might have been mentioned that the birds are more buoyant and not as chesty as Poms, that most Parasitics have 3 to 5 white-shafted primaries (usually 2 in Long-tailed and 5 to 7 in Pomarine), and that they have narrower wings than Poms, especially near the body. Some immature Parasitics have cinnamon coloration, unique to the species. Along the west coast Parasitics are generally the nearshore jaeger, pirating small gulls and terns.

POMARINE JAEGER – On page 139 there should be a heavier dark breast band, either heavily spotted (probably males) or solid black (probably females). White-chested adults occur but are scarce.
Text: On page 138 it might have been mentioned that this is the bulkiest jaeger with the largest white splash in the outer wing (see under Parasitic Jaeger). The wings themselves are

broader than the smaller jaegers', particularly near the base. Along the west coast Poms are most often encountered over relatively shallow water but definitely offshore, harassing shearwaters.

LONG-TAILED JAEGER – **Text**: It might be mentioned that this is the most buoyant jaeger with the narrowest wings. Usually only the two outermost primaries are white-shafted. This is the grayest jaeger in any age (especially useful in determining juveniles), and all age birds have a blackish trailing edge which contrasts with the mantle (this is illustrated for adults but not enunciated). Along the west coast Long-taileds migrate more seaward than most Parasitics and Poms, along the corridor used by Arctic Terns which are their providers.

GREAT SKUA – On page 139 the flying bird looks like an illustration of a juvenile South Polar Skua. **In Life** Great Skua has ruddy reddish hues and is extensively striped.
Map: On page 138 the map next to Great Skua shows winter range in the Pacific north to British Columbia. Because there are no North Pacific records, they must mean this to be South Polar Skua, but there are two things wrong. First, South Polar Skua also occurs in the northwestern Atlantic, and maybe some of that blue ink refers to them. Second, the species is regular in fall, rare in spring and practically unheard of winter so there should be red hatching, not solid blue. Some of the blue must really mean Great Skua since they are known to occur in the far northwestern Atlantic in winter. It is unclear what is being said on this map, but if the attempt is to illustrate ranges of two species it would be nice if that were mentioned. Note also that the new edition has expanded the inch dimensions from the old edition. A Skua with the latter shape would have a lot of trouble staying airborne.

IVORY GULL – **Map**: On page 140 add that the Ivory Gull occurs along the arctic coast of Alaska and in the Bering and Chuckchi Seas which aren't even on the map.

GLAUCOUS GULL – On page 141 the bills of both first and second winter individuals are not good, and the second-winter bird is too white. **In Life** the basal two-thirds of the bill is bright pink and the distal one-third sharply black. Early second-winter birds have extensive brown flecking, and later ones have gray backs.
Text: Add that first winter birds become very white and unpatterned as spring approaches. Add that first winter birds of both this species and Iceland Gull have marbling on the dorsal tail surface. Same aged Glaucous-winged and Thayer's Gulls have largely unpatterned solid gray dorsal tail surfaces.
Note: Some Alaskan birds and those which occur along the west coast in winter are really small compared to Atlantic ones which are of the large, nominate race. Thus the identification of Iceland Gull becomes more difficult. Shape is the best early clue, Icelands being small-billed, round-headed, with skinny legs and with primaries that project more than a bill length beyond the tail tip. In the first year of life Iceland would have a darker bill than equal age Glaucous.

GLAUCOUS-WINGED GULL – On page 141 the juvenile is too dark gray and has the wrong color legs. **In Life** the bird is more sandy brown and the leg and foot are pink not black. In the adults note that white *secondaries* are not an I.D. factor from Glaucous Gull as shown.
Text: On page 141 add that when perched, the stacking and shadowing of the primary feathers can make the wingtips *look* nearly black. Add also that Glaucous-winged X Western hybrids are abundant in Puget Sound (where they are jokingly called Larus pugetensis) and farther down the coast in winter. Add that winter adults are heavily streaked on the nape and neck. Some are so heavy as to appear hooded with streaks.

GREAT BLACK-BACKED GULL – On page 143 the second-winter bird should have some black in the back, and the first-winter bird should appear more checkered.

SLATY-BACKED GULL – On page 143 the wingtips are wrong and the white trailing edge to the wing is too narrow. **In Life** the outer primary tips are black and contrast the dark gray mantle. Blacken them in. This fact is true also of Western Gull and Lesser Black-backed and causes some mis-identifications. Also the white trailing edge of the secondaries is wider than is shown and is very obvious. When perched, these white tips show as a bold white patch on each side of the mantle.
Text: Add that the Siberiasian race of Herring Gull (*L. a. vegae*) occurs regularly in western Alaska (more frequently than Slaty-backs) and is much darker-mantled than Herring Gulls in the rest of North America. Also note that most gulls, even Kittiwakes and Glaucous Gulls, appear dark-mantled when perched on ice or snow. Also, iris color in Western Gull is highly variable (gold, yellow, even white), so this feature is not a field mark.

WESTERN GULL – On page 143 the picture of the flying adult has the wrong wingtips. **In Life** Western Gulls have black primary sub-tips which sharply contrast the gray mantle. This is more evident in the northern race (*L. o. occidentalis*) which is paler-mantled than the southern race (*L. o. wymanii*), but all Westerns show it. Blacken them in.
Text: Add that adult Western Gulls' heads remain immaculate in winter (slightly dusky edgings in some *wymanii*) while all other west coast gulls (except adult Glaucous) in winter have obvious gray nape and neck streaks.
Map: The pink spot out there in the desert west and north of Great Salt Lake must be a spill since Western Gulls do not breed in central Utah!! Add that they winter inside the Gulf of California as far north as Loreto.

YELLOW-FOOTED GULL – **Text:** On page 142 only full adults have bright yellow legs. Note that unlike most North American big gulls, *livens* has only three winter plumages to adulthood. Most others have four. First winter *livens* have mostly white (not mottled) underparts.

LESSER BLACK-BACKED GULL – On page 142 the wing-tips of the flying adult have the wrong pattern. **In Life** the primary sub-tips are black and contrast the medium gray mantle. Also, only the longest primary has a sub-apical white spot. The others are dark.
Text: It should be mentioned that Lesser Black-backeds have longer primaries than the other dark-mantled gulls and are shaped more like Californias than Great Black-backeds.

LARGE AND MEDIUM GRAY-BACKED, WHITE-HEADED GULLS – GENERAL – On pages 145 and 147 the mantle (back and dorsal surface of the wings) colors are misleading. Although the new text tries to explain the problem, the pictures are still off. The gray of Herring and Ring-billed should be the same and pale (like the gray of adult Common Black-headed Gull on page 149); that of Thayer's and Mew should be notably darker; and that of California should be clearly darker than any of the preceding (more like that of Western Gull as illustrated on page 143). Also, adults of all these species (Herring, Thayer's, California, Ring-billed and Mew) have dusky nape streaks in winter.

HERRING GULL – **Text:** On page 144 it should be said that some first winter birds have pinkish-based bills to various degrees, especially Pacific birds. Also, though the text compares a number of species to adult and to first- and second-year Herrings, the *real* look-alikes are not mentioned. Ring-billeds, Californias, Lesser and Great Black-backeds are not really similar compared to Thayer's and Westerns. (See under Thayer's Gull, and add that first winter Thayer's look most like first winter Glaucous-winged Gulls but have Hershey Bar primaries which contrast the tan, marbled wing coverts and back.) First winter Westerns are very like same aged Herrings but are more sooty gray (less warm brown) and are more highly patterned especially on the back and rump. First winter Herrings show a pale window on the inner primaries unlike equal-age Westerns and Californias.

THAYER'S GULL – On page 144 note that the iris of adults may be very light. Also it should be known that from southern British Columbia to central California numerous Western x Glaucous-winged hybrids are found in winter and they often have the markings of Thayer's Gull. At this point, the observer must rely on proportions and dead reckoning. Thayer's seldom occur with numbers of Westerns or Glaucous-wingeds, but the hybrids always do. Herring x Glaucous-winged hybrids are also Thayer's lookalikes. These illustrations may be counter-helpful.

CALIFORNIA GULL – On page 144 the mantle shade is too light and the first winter bird's bill is too dark. **In Life** the mantle is much darker than Herring's and noticeably darker than Thayer's. Also, the bill of first winter birds is bright pink for the basal two-thirds and sharply black for the distal one-third. Also, California's unique posture should be illustrated. They often lean back the shoulders to a point where the primaries seem to practically drag on the ground.
Text: Add that adults have much gray streaking on the nape in winter. Also note legs and feet of this species are seldom yellow (as they are on Ring-billed and Mew) and are most often greenish or pale blue, orange in spring.

RING-BILLED GULL – On page 147 the mantle is too dark and an important plumage is not shown. **In Life** the mantle is clearly paler than that of Mew Gull and a lot paler than that of California (page 145). Also the second winter plumage is like that of an adult, including entirely white head and tail, but lacks white apical spots in the black primary tips and has been mistaken for Black-legged Kittiwake. It is no wonder, since books suggest that Kittiwake is the only gull with solid black. This plumage should have been shown and the Kittiwake business described. Shape: see under Mew Gull below.

MEW GULL – **Text**: On page 146 add that Mews with less black in the wingtips also have *more white* there! Also, the small bill, rounded head and large, dark eye give all ages a gentle look to the face which, when learned, will identify the species. Also both this and Ring-billed Gulls have very long primary feathers which give them a unique streamlined look when perched.

LAUGHING GULL – On page 149 the "im." is a juvenile and is too dark. Also, winter adults and second-winter birds have a dark smudge behind the eye, not a speckled look to the head as shown uppermost left.

FRANKLIN'S GULL – **Text**: On page 148 the third sentence is new and correct and prompted the new and correct picture of the flying immature with an all white outer tail feather on page 149. Also, on page 150 under "immature gulls"–oops! the Franklin's again has a black-banded outer tail feather.

SABINE'S GULL – On page 149 the flying immature is too uniform. *Actually* the back and innerwing feathers are pale-edged making a beautiful scaly pattern.

COMMON BLACK-HEADED GULL – On page 149 the hood of the "summer" bird is slightly the wrong shape and the colors of the immature's soft parts are wrong. **In Life** the species is not as black-headed as Bonaparte's or Little Gull and is more black-faced with the black crossing the head above and behind the eye. The nape is white. The "black" head is really brown. First-winter birds have pink to reddish legs and feet and red, not yellow, bases to the bill.

ARCTIC TERN – On page 153 the shape of this and Common Tern are too similar. **In Life** Arctic has a short bill, round head, short neck and long tail, making that part of the bird aft of the trailing edge of the wings longer than that part in front of the leading edge. Common has a longer bill, flatter head and longer neck as well as a relatively shorter tail, making the amounts of bird before and behind the wings more equal.

COMMON TERN – On page 153, give the standing adult gray underparts as is true in summer, to help prevent folks from calling breeding adult Commons, Arctic.
Text: On page 152 the map is new. In previous editions, the common presence of this species on the west coast was not acknowledged. The bird does not, however, winter in northern Baja.
Map: On page 162 note that common Tern in winter in southern California and northern Baja is so rare that the blue color here is misleading.

ELEGANT TERN – On page 155 the wingtips are too pale on both flying and sitting birds and the face pattern for the winter bird is not quite right. **In Life** during much of the year Elegant's primary feathers show quite blackish and can be told from the pale primaries of Royal both in flight and while sitting. (Elegants in fresh plumage are at their palest, while worn Royals are at their darkest.) Also, the sitting bird should have the eye wholly included in the black (like the picture of Royal Tern). Conversely, Royals have the eye isolated in the white. The head patterns are reversed in the guide.
Text: It should be mentioned that high plumaged birds have a pink blush below. Also the bills of immatures are yellow, not blackish.

ROYAL TERN – On page 155 the face pattern is wrong, at least for western Royals. **In Life** the eye is isolated in the

white part of the face (even more so than the picture of Elegant Tern).
Map: On page 154 the winter range extends too far up the west coast. In recent years the species has become exceptional north of Morro Bay.

CASPIAN TERN – On page 155 the underwings are too pale and the bills lack a critical feature. **In Life** Caspians have nearly black ventral primary surfaces which easily identify them from flying Royals. Also the bills of most Caspians have grayish tip including perhaps one-quarter of the bill or at least the culmen at the tip. Elegant and Royal Terns have orange bills with no dark on the tips.

BLACK SKIMMER – **Map:** On page 156 the species is resident from San Diego down the west coast of Baja and on the gulf side north to La Paz and is usual and nests sporadically at the Salton Sea.

IMMATURE TERNS – On page 158 and 159 the Caspian Tern should have buffy scallops on the back and wing coverts; these are remnants of juvenal plumage and are worn into the first winter. The Common Terns both show the narrow trailing edge to the primaries *typical* of Arctic Tern. The Arctic Terns' heads and especially bills are too large. The Least Tern should be about 25 percent smaller.

COMMON MURRE – On page 161 the birds are too slaty black. **In Life** they are dark velvety brown becoming more pallid with wear and can be told from fresh plumaged Thick-billed Murres (which are black), especially in flight.

THICK-BILLED MURRE – **Text:** The sixth through eighth words in the second sentence are new and important for diagnosis.

BLACK GUILLEMOT – On page 161 another illustration

would complete the picture. **In Life** flying Black Guillemots have flashy, silvery white underwings while Pigeon Guillemots have dark underwings. By far the easiest way to separate the species, this calls out to be illustrated. It is not even mentioned.
Text: The last two words seem unnecessary. All alcids beat their wings quickly and the statement is of no use for identification.

PIGEON GUILLEMOT – On page 161 the underwings of this and Black Guillemot needed to be shown. **In Life** Pigeons' underwings are dusky with a smudgy white core, while Blacks' are uniform silvery white. This is the best mark and really should be pointed out.

CASSIN'S AUKLET – On page 165 the flying bird is too dark-bellied and all are a bit too gray. **In Life** Cassin's Auklets have very white bellies, easily seen as they twist and turn in flight. Also, the species' basic color is dark brown, not grayish-purple as in my copy.
Text: The second word is unnecessary since it does not occur onshore away from island colonies.

MARBLED MURRELET – On page 165 the summer bird should be more generally marbled.

KITTLITZ'S MURRELET – On page 165 the summer bird is too dark. **In Life** these birds are sandy yellow in color.
Text: A very good feature and sometimes the only usable mark (when they are taking off or landing) are Kittlitz's' white outer tail feathers. They should have been mentioned.

XANTUS' MURRELET – On page 165 the picture of the sitting bird is too squat. **In Life** Xantus' and Craveri's, but no other murrelets, usually swim with the head high on erect necks. Also, there are two easily identifiable forms which should be kept track of pending future taxonomic revisions; see illustration.

CRAVERI'S MURRELET – Too bad this species is not pictured. They are regular and sometimes common off of California north to Monterey in late summer and early fall. **In Life** Craveri's is blacker than Xantus' with the black of the face usually lower and connecting on the chin. The intrusion of black from the upper back onto the white chest is more evident than on Xantus' and shows in flight. Also the underwings are dusky but usually with a strong white core. (The underwings of Xantus' are entirely white.) It is important to know differences other than underwings, since the birds usually skitter off very low to the water. Often as a boat approaches, a bird will stretch its wings nervously, revealing the pattern. So be watching. Like Xantus' but not other murrelets, Craveri's usually swims with head high on an extended neck.

ANCIENT MURRELET – On page 165 the birds are not contrasty enough and the bills are too dull. **In Life** all year the back is really pale gray and very sharply different from the black crown. The bill is bright yellow and noticeable at a fair distance. This species swims scrunched down (as in the illustration). See Xantus' Murrelet above.

RED-BILLED PIGEON – On page 167 note that the bills of many of this species are mostly yellow.

SPOTTED DOVE – **Text**: On page 168 add that it also occurs in Bakersfield and is common in residential Indio near the Salton Sea.

INCA DOVE – **Text**: On page 168 its endless call has been said as "no-hope, no-hope" in English, and it is a good remember trick.

WHITE-TIPPED DOVE – **Text:** On page 168 the last three words, in parentheses, are new and very appropriate. It is one of those bird voices that may be going on nearby but is practically unnoticeable.

WESTERN SCREECH OWL – **Text:** On page 174 voices also include a double trill with the longer, second part descending and a crisply spoken alarm note "took-took."

LONG-EARED OWL – **Text:** On page 174 add that this species and the Short-eared Owl fly very much the same and very differently from any other North American owl. The flaps are very high and deep like those of giant, slow motion moths. It seems at times that the wingtips are staying still and the body is pulsing up and down. Also, Long-eareds are gray brown, Short-eareds buffy brown.

SHORT-EARED OWL – **Text:** On page 174 the unique flight might well have been described. See Long-eared Owl above.

BARN OWL – **Text:** On page 176 the fifth word does not apply in the far west and southwest. **In Life** Barn Owls are common (for an owl) in unforested areas of many western states like Oregon, California, Nevada and Arizona.

BARRED OWL – **Text:** On page 176 add that the voice has been interpreted as saying "who-cooks, who-cooks, who-cooks-for-you." This is very good common knowledge and easy to remember. White-winged Dove can say the same thing in the same voice with only half as many notes.
Map: This species is spreading, occurs year-round in Washington, Oregon and northern California, and nobody was trying to keep that a secret.

SPOTTED OWL – **Text:** On page 176 the second word of text is misleading and more should perhaps be said about the voice. **In Life** Spotted Owls are actually fairly common throughout their range in proper habitat. Add that the loud voice in English could be "whoo, who-are-you" or "Hoo Hoo . . . Hooooo," dropping off sharply at the end. Also puppy-like barking for as many as ten barks on the same pitch and a loud rising hummed-whistle is sometimes heard.

SAW-WHET OWL – **Text:** On page 178 add at the end that the rhythm of calls in series is much faster (up to two per second) and slightly higher than Northern Pygmy Owl. Also there is a blood-curdling "weeeeek," ascending towards the end and a sharp, growled "taugh" used for alarm.
Map: Resident range in California and Nevada is much more widespread than shown.

FLAMMULATED OWL – **Text:** On page 180 add that the basic call is a very resonant "hoop" or "hoop-oop." Also add that they usually call from a perch very near the trunk of a large tree and that they are master ventriloquists often sounding farther away than they really are.

NORTHERN PYGMY OWL – **Text:** On page 180 add that the call is a single, whistled "hoo" in series ten to twenty per minute. The "hoo" is doubled by Northern Pygmies in the mountains of southeast Arizona, southwest New Mexico, and in the Sierra Madre Occidental.

COMMON POORWILL – **Text:** On page 182 add that the voice is a mellow, resonant "who-will, who-will" with a sharp upward inflection on the "will." If close and quiet an observer may hear a grace note at the end of each doubled call.

LESSER NIGHTHAWK – **Map:** On page 182 add purple in the southern half of Baja where these birds are abundant in winter!

VAUX'S SWIFT (say Vawks) – On page 185 the flying bird is too white on the underparts. **In Life** the birds are almost

White-throated Swift

uniform mouse brown on the underparts, slightly paler on the chin.
Text: Add that Chimney Swifts do a lot of soaring while Vaux's is almost always twinkling.
Map: This species does not winter regularly in coastal Texas and Louisiana.

WHITE-THROATED SWIFT – On page 185 the tails (though correct) are not the way they usually appear. **In Life** the outer feathers are drawn together and the whole tail looks spine-like.
Text: Add that the voice is a long, roller coastering "te-ti-ti-ti-te-te-te" and that in one sequence can sound much like the opening song of a Canyon Wren.

RUBY-THROATED HUMMINGBIRD – **Map:** On page 186 it is likely that most if not all *Archilochus* hummers wintering in southern Florida are Black-chinneds, not Ruby-throateds.

BROAD-TAILED HUMMINGBIRD – On page 187 the perched female shows way too much orange in the base of the outer tail feathers and thus looks like an Allen's or Rufous.
Text: On page 186 the first part of the third sentence is new. These young males, almost a full year old, may have fully red gorgets but do not buzz in flight and could be mistaken for Ruby-throated Hummingbirds.
Map: The breeding range in California is much too extensive. These birds occupy a very narrow strip of mountainous habitat entirely *east* of the Sierra Nevada.

CALLIOPE HUMMINGBIRD – **Map:** On page 186 the breeding range is much too extensive. Actually, most breed in the high Cascades and eastern escarpment of the Sierra, not in central valleys and not along the coast–even in Washington!

Lucifer Hummingbird

COSTA'S HUMMINGBIRD – **Map:** On page 188 the bird nests only in xeric habitats and is very local in the U.S. in winter. Also the last sentence of text for this and for Black-chinned Hummingbird are new and from us.

LUCIFER HUMMINGBIRD – On page 191 the male lacks a prominent field mark and the female could be brighter. **In Life** males have bright buffy flanks. Females and especially fledglings are quite orange below. Also, males usually perch and fly with the outer retrices closed to a point. They are spine-tailed looking rather than fork-tailed.

BLUE-THROATED HUMMINGBIRD – On page 191 the bills of both birds are shown relatively as long as those of Magnificent Hummingbird, and the underparts of the male are shown as green. **In Life** Blue-throated's bill is much shorter than Magnificent's and is only slightly longer than the head. The underparts of the male are gray, not green.

BERYLLINE HUMMINGBIRD ***(Amazilia beryllina)*** – On page 190 this species is *altogether missing!!* It is seen most years in late summer and early fall in canyons of southeast Arizona and has nested on at least two occasions. It is like the Buff-bellied Hummingbird pictured on page 191 but the belly is more grayish and the wings are iridescent copper-maroon. It has a squared tail (not clearly forked as Buff-bellieds have **in life** but not in the illustration). The amount of green on the underparts varies with age and gender. They are bulky, medium-sized hummers. The song of Berylline is unique and may sound like an arboreal gnome playing a kazoo.

ELEGANT TROGON – On page 193 the pictures are misinforming in two ways. We've heard several people express surprise at how big trogons *really* are when seen for the first time. From this picture and sizes relative to kingfishers they had expected a bird about the size of a grosbeak. **In Life**

Elegant Trogons are *big* birds. Their bodies are certainly near the size of Belted Kingfisher bodies and their tails are much longer. Also, the illustration of the male is positioned in such a way that to some people the tail surface appears to be the ventral. **In Life** that which is drawn is the dorsal surface. The ventral surface of the male's tail is very similar to that shown for the female.

PILEATED WOODPECKER – Text: Add at the end that the primary call is like the long call of Common Flicker but is a bigger sound and is more ringing. It might be written as 'ca-ca-ca-ca-ca-ca-ca-ca'' quieting and dropping slightly towards the end.

LADDER-BACKED WOODPECKER – Text: On page 196 the last word is new, different and more correct than former editions.

NUTTALL'S WOODPECKER – Text: On page 196 the whole last sentence is new, accurate and very helpful for identification. For fun, compare this to the voice description from any earlier issue.

LEWIS' WOODPECKER – Text: On page 198 replace the last sentence with "Call like that of Hairy Woodpecker but muted; also like that of Groove-billed Ani."

ACORN WOODPECKER – On page 199 the bird pictured is a male and the female should be shown or mentioned somewhere. The female has a broad dark bar which separates the red crown from the yellow-white forecrown.
Text: The last sentence is new and good. For fun compare these words to those they replaced. Also in the text it would be well to mention that birds of this species are accomplished flycatchers as well as acorn farmers.

SPHYRAPICUS SAPSUCKERS – Text: On page 198 the last

sentence under Yellow-bellied isn't really very helpful. Add that the calls of all populations are rather loud, nasal "wheeers" or series of same (like Sharp-shinned Hawk). An easy way to remember which races have become which species is that the red-hooded ones are Red-breasteds while the black-and-white-faced ones are Yellow-bellieds. Easier yet, remember stripes and solids. One or two more separate species may be extracted from this complex.

WILLIAMSON'S SAPSUCKER – **Text:** On page 198 add that in the nesting season and occasionally at other times of the year the territorial statement can identify this species. It is a snare drum-like drill, fast-slow-fast-slow, like Morse Code.

HAIRY WOODPECKER – **Text:** On page 200 (or 201 in a picture) it should be mentioned that some western races have nearly totally black wings, lacking white spots.

BLACK-BACKED WOODPECKER – On page 201 the bill is too small. **In Life** the bill is relatively much longer and deeper than in Three-toed Woodpecker.

THREE-TOED WOODPECKER – On page 201 the back pattern varies geographically. **In Life** the back can be nearly solid white like Hairy Woodpecker's, or nearly lacking any white pattern like a Black-backed's.

ROSE-THROATED BECARD – On page 205 the female's tail is too dull. **In Life** the tail is bright orange contrasting the flat browns of the rest of the plumage.
Text: The last sentence is not what I hear from these birds. I have whited that out and replaced it with "Call a very high, wiry noise. Short, wheezy and slightly descending."

SULPHUR-BELLIED FLYCATCHER – On page 205 the face pattern and the tail are too dull. **In Life** the dark auriculars (ear coverts) are bordered by prominent white stripes.

Sulphur-bellied Flycatcher

The dorsal tail surface is bright orange, more so than any Myiarchus flycatcher.
Text: The last sentence is very misleading. To me this species sounds nothing like a Western Flycatcher except perhaps that they are both birds! While Western Flycatcher is quiet, staccato and rhythmic, the voice of Sulphur-bellies is a long, squealy, spewing rubber duck noise sharply descending near the end.

TROPICAL KINGBIRD – On page 207 the tail is too dark. **In Life** both this species and Couch's Kingbird have mouse brown to pale brown tails depending upon wear.
Text: On page 206 the last sentence under Tropical Kingbird (above Couch's Kingbird) is not representative of what members of that species sound like. I have replaced that statement with "No! high, metallic trills."

THICK-BILLED KINGBIRD – On page 107 the crown, face and nape are too dark and the tail tip is the wrong shape. **In Life** the cap including the face is gray-brown but pale enough that the black auricular patch is distinct. Also, the tails of real TBKBs are not rounded as shown but are notched like the neighboring picture of the tail of Gray Kingbird.

Text: On page 206 the last sentence is new and informative. Also add that the call may be written as "peez-zeeer," wheezy and dropping.

DUSKY-CAPPED FLYCATCHER – On page 209 the face of sitting bird is wrong. **In Life** these birds are very bushy-headed (even the forecrown) and *do not have white eyerings.* Also they are clearly the yellowest-bellied Myiarchus after Great-crested. The illustration of the leaf gleaning bird is much more realistic than the perched one.
Text: At the end add that the call is like Say's Phoebe but even clearer.

BLACK PHOEBE – On page 211 you may want to write in that juveniles have tan to whitish wingbars into the first winter.
Text:Add at the end that the usual call note is very similar to that of Swamp Sparrow.

SAY'S PHOEBE – **Text**: On page 210 add that the call has the quality of part of the call of Black-bellied Plover and is much like that of Dusky-capped Flycatcher but slightly windier.

EMPIDONAX FLYCATCHERS – Many of us grew up being told by authorities that non-singing Empidonaces were unidentifiable in the field, and up until about fifteen years ago, most of us believed it. Because most species of Empidonax only sing on the breeding territory (but call throughout the rest of the year) it seemed reasonable to search for identification traits *other than song.* Thus, recently, methods have been developed to such a critical level that for those who learn them even silent individual birds on migration can mostly be identified given a decent study.

In most field guides, including those which use photographs and including the Golden Guide, some species are so poorly represented that the pictures are counter-helpful. The subject is huge and deserves a major dissertation. All we can do here in this regard is drop some hints to make the book (more) useful. While consulting on changes needed for the expanded, revised edition we pointed out the obvious: that the pictures were more a problem than the text. When told that it would not be possible to re-do the plates, we asked for at least a crack at the flycatchers. They complied and sent proofs which were returned with innumerable suggestions for making them right. Of all the suggestions, it appears the only one utilized was to splash a little yellow paint in the vicinity of the underparts of Hammond's and Western Flycatchers. With accurate information in hand, somebody chose to go with the old, incorrect plates anyway, ho hum.

In general, the eastern species have more and wider pale edges to the inner secondaries and tertials than western species do. The inner secondaries and tertials themselves are more dark-centered than in western species making for more striking contrasts. Some species have almond shaped eyerings, some have almost round eyerings, and some have no eyerings at all. Some call a soft "whit," some a sharp "peet," and some do otherwise. Some look big-headed and short-tailed, some look normal headed and long-tailed.

YELLOW-BELLIED FLYCATCHER – On page 213 the pictures are pretty good. The eyering is nearly round, the wingbars are white and yellow, and there are bold white edges to the inner secondaries. However, the crown and back color in my copy are a bit dull for fresh plumaged birds, and the lores seem wrong. **In Life** fresh plumaged birds, especially juveniles, have medium green backs and forest green crowns containing tiny black streaks. Also, the eyering is discreet on the greenish face without the loreal line connecting it to the base of the bill as shown. They are *not* spectacled.

ACADIAN FLYCATCHER – On page 213 the bird seems too uniform and not bright enough for fresh plumaged birds. **In Life** many are white from the chin all the way ventrally to

the under tail coverts but with broad yellowish sides and flanks. The backs of fresh individuals are definitely olive (not brown) and the bill is huge for an Empid–like Western's, Alder's or Willow's but much bigger than all the others'. The eyering is white but the wingbars are creamy.
Text: On page 212 no mention is made of the call note. It has been reliably said that the note is a sharp, almost explosive "peep."

WILLOW FLYCATCHER – On page 213 there is a real problem. The illustration does not look like a Willow Flycatcher or an Alder Flycatcher! The one shown has a sharply defined white throat, has a very dark-capped look and has a big white eyering. **In Life** Willow Flycatchers are more uniform whitish (but not white) on the throat and breast, yellowing slightly on the belly. The breast is entirely dusted with brownish, not sharply delineated from throat or belly. The upperparts are uniform medium brown (not dark brown-capped). Also, real life Willows do not have obvious light eyerings and for this reason may be more easily mistaken for Pewees than for other members of their genus.
Text: On page 212 add that this species seldom flips its tail and that the call note, frequently given on migration, is a soft, liquid "whit."

ALDER FLYCATCHER – On page 213 the illustration is inadequate to identify the species (see above under Willow Flycatcher). **In Life** Alders look very much like Willows with a slightly greener cast to the back and a barely perceptible white eyring. Both are large and long-tailed, uniform brownish (olive-gray in fresh Alders) above and dusty below with very large bills, orange ventrally.
Text: On page 212 it is well stated that the quality of Alder and Willow Flycatchers' songs are similar. In fact, they sound *very* much the same. The popular written words for the songs, "fitz-bew" for the Willow and "wee-bee-o" for Alder suggest that they are more different than they really are. Add

that Alder's *call* given on migration and on the breeding grounds is a soft "whip." Vocalizations *are* the best way to tell the two "Traill's" apart.

LEAST FLYCATCHER – On page 213 the illustration is correct for shape (small bill, big head and short tail) but the species is quite variable in plumage and needs discussion. **In Life** most Leasts are lighter below than the illustration, some being white-throated *and -chested.* The upperparts are brownish gray (less brown than Willow Flycatcher). The eyering is bold and almond shaped and *lacks* the line (shown) connecting it to the bill.
Text: Add that the call note given frequently during migration and on the wintering grounds is a rather crisp "chit," a bit flatter than the soft "whit" of Willow and Dusky Flycatchers but noticeably more mellow than the sharp "pik" notes of Alder and Hammond's.

HAMMOND'S FLYCATCHER – On page 215 the bird on the right is too uniform below, has too gray a back, has pale lores and a bicolored bill. **In Life** there is a grayish olive wash across the breast between the light gray throat and *pale* yellow belly. The back is greenish, the lores are gray as is the rest of the face, and the bill is nearlv entirely black. The shape of this bird is good, being large-headed and short-tailed. The bill is very small (the smallest of Empidonax flycatchers). Hammond's do lot of nervous tail and wing flicking, and because of their even white eyering, small bill and wingbars may remind one of Ruby-crowned Kinglet when in fresh plumage. The same things apply to the bird on the left plus the fact that the yellow belly here is much too bright.
Text: The last sentence is new. The only other Empid that has a sharp "peak" or "pic" note is Alder. This note sounds like the beginning notes in Pgymy Nutchatch twitter and is very unlike the call notes of other Empids. The most often heard summer voice is an abrupt 'tse-beak," similar to the

voice of Least Flycatcher. See below for Hammonds'/Dusky differences.

DUSKY FLYCATCHER – On page 215 the bird is too uniform for a fresh plumaged bird. Like Hammond's, **In Life** there is a grayish wash across the breast (though often paler than Hammond's) which separates the whitish throat from the pale yellow belly. The back is olive green which contrasts the olive brown crown (usually less contrasty than similar plumaged Hammond's). Though Hammond's and Dusky are very similar several points differ consistently. (1) *Call note.* Hammond's "pic" or "peak"; Dusky a soft, sharp "whit." (2) *Shape.* Hammond's is large-headed and short-tailed while Dusky is normal headed and long-tailed. (That distinction takes practice.) (3) *Bill.* Hammond's bill is tiny. Dusky's bill, though smaller than most Empidonax, is longer than Hammond's and looks proportionately correct on its face. (4) *Tail.* In fresh plumage Hammond's tail is uniform brown throughout (though the outer web of the outer feather looks paler tan because it is a single layer). Dusky's outer web to the outer tail feather is whitish (but not so sharply contrasting as that of Gray Flycatcher). (5) *Behavior.* During migration Hammond's is much more twitchy, often flicking up its tail and simultaneously flitting its wings. Duskies are mostly more sedate, flicking the tail (not so often wings) once or twice after perching then remaining relatively still. This is not a diagnostic feature, just a hint, and only works away from nesting areas. Both species are very twitchy while on territory. The most often heard voice in summer is doubled and moves like the opening two notes of the Mexican Hat Dance.

GRAY FLYCATCHER – On page 215 the eyering is too dull and the tail too short. **In Life** Grays have a clear, round white eyering, the only break in the *pale gray* face, nape and back. The tail is long and in addition to the fact that this is the only Empid which begins the tail movement with a downstroke, the whole tail is floppy (less rigid than the tails of any other species) and looks like it may blow away in the breeze. Many Grays are nearly all white below with a tinge of yellow on the belly. All Grays have a distinctly *pink* or *orange* lower mandible which is dark at the tip. Outer web of outer tail feather is white.

Text: Add at the end that the call is a quick, soft "wit" like Dusky's but sharper.

Map: Though they are sparse winterers from southeast Arizona south (rarely to NW Oaxaca), they are abundant then in the Cape region of Baja, their winter stronghold.

WESTERN FLYCATCHER – On page 215 the eyering is wrong, the yellow below is too dark and in the wrong places, the wingbars are the wrong color for most individuals, and if the illustration is supposed to represent fresh plumage, the crown, nape, face and back color are mistaken. **In Life** all age Western Flycatchers have large, almond shaped eyerings (not small round ones) isolated on the darker face. There simply is no white line through the lores connecting the eyering to the base of the bill as is shown. The illustration shows spectacles and is very misleading. The yellow below should be paler (especially for northwestern and Channel Island birds) and should be more uniformly distributed. The patchy color below may be, in part, my fault.

While attempting to point out what was wrong with the plates I suggested that the underparts of fresh plumaged Western Flycatchers should be "uniformly pale yellow" and tried to indicate it as in the illustration on the top of the next page. Apparently that was interpreted as uniform yellow on the throat and belly, leaving the breast gray as in previous editions!!

Anyway, to press on, the wingbars **In Life** are tan or dull yellowish but white only on worn, fall adults. The crown, nape, face and back are green (autumn adults can be quite brown backed and white below due to wear). The bill is very large and wide and the lower mandible is orange.

Text: Add at the end that the call note for the female is a

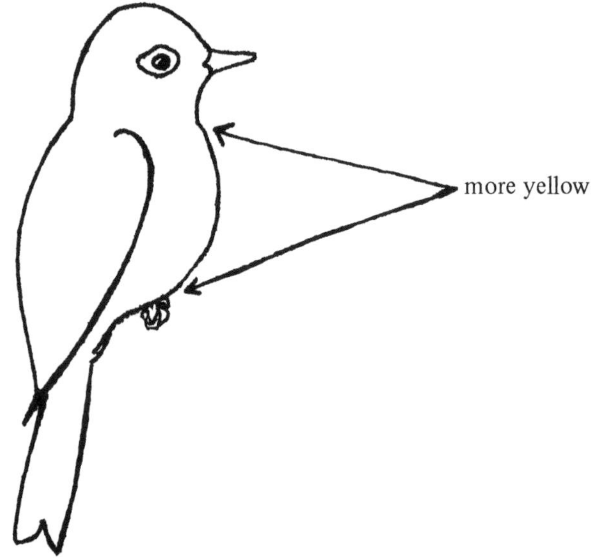

very, very high "zzt" (Creeper quality but short) and is a common vocalization during migration and in winter. Males give the "pseeit" or "pit-peet" which is considered to be the song mostly in spring and summer. If it says "whit" it is not a Western.

BUFF-BREASTED FLYCATCHER – On page 215 it's the same old problem. The bird has the wrong eyering and facial markings and the lower mandible is too dark. **In Life** the eye-ring is more evident and the lores are slightly paler than the cheek–but they are not spectacled. Also, this species has a distinct orangy lower mandible. Immatures are brighter orange breasted than the bird shown.

NORTHERN BEARDLESS TYRANNULET – On page 215 the head is too round, the bill is too big, and the facial markings are wrong. **In Life** these birds are really cresty, that is, all the crown feathers, though not long, are almost always held erected. Perhaps because of this crestness the bill looks more petite than the illustration shows. This species has a subtle

Western Flycatcher

face pattern but one that gives it a distinctive look. There is a whitish superciliary (eyebrow) which is not sharply defined (and is like Warbling Vireo's) and there is a fairly distinct under-eyering. These features give the bird in life a very different expression from the one shown. This picture has the same mistakes as the illustrations by Peterson in his Western Field Guide.

GREATER PEWEE ("jumbo shrimp?") – On page 217 the bird's crown is too rounded and the birds are too brown. **In Life** this species is really cresty and almost tufted. Worn birds are quite uniform gray, darker above but not brown. Fresh autumn birds have a distinct yellow cast below and are more olive above. On live birds the mandible is pink or orange rather than yellow.
Text: The last sentence is misstated. The italicized words are the bird's song, not call. *Add* that the call is a staccato "pit-pit."
Map: The bird is extremely rare in the U.S. in winter. There is not a wintering area in southeastern California as shown.

PEWEES – On page 217 the illustrations are relatively good with Western being sootier (it often appears open-vested like an Olive-sided) and darker-backed. It should be mentioned somewhere that some Westerns (especially juveniles) have nearly all orange lower mandibles and it is not a conclusive mark for Eastern. Also *except for full song* many vocalizations are shared by both species.

OLIVE-SIDED FLYCATCHER – **Text**: On page 216 the English interpretation for the song does not work on western populations. The experts have been talking about "quick-three-beers" or the like for fifty years or so. That suggests to me that the first two notes are on the same pitch and the third is a bit lower. For me, growing up in California, *my* Olive-sided Flycatchers didn't say that but said "I say there" with the middle note much higher and the last note slightly lower than the first. The trouble didn't come clear until I heard an Eastern one. The two songs are noticeably different.

HORNED LARK – On page 219 note that juvenal plumage (worn for several weeks after fledging) is very patterned and is very streaky brown and tan above and below. At that stage larks might be mistaken for pipits or even basic-plumaged longspurs.

CAVE SWALLOW – **Text:** On page 218 the last two words in the second sentence are new and very helpful. Looking up at a swarm of swallows (after the exodus from a nesting culvert) it is very difficult to spot a buffy throat. Of the "square-tailed swallows" the flight feathers of Cave are slightly translucent while those of Cliff are opaque. Barn Swallows' are opaque too.

Another note of use in the field is that Cave Swallow's nest is not a mud gourd like Cliff Swallow's but is an open mud cup much like a Barn Swallow's but with an inch-wide porch around the rim. In artificial nesting spots (culverts) Cave Swallows seldom cohabit with Cliffs but often do with Barns, and Barn x Cave hybrids are known. Extralimitally (in Arizona) Cave Swallows have used vacant Cliff Swallow nests.

VIOLET-GREEN SWALLOW – On page 221 the adult is too dull and the tail is too long. **In Life** adult male Violet-green Swallows are stunningly beautiful with their brilliant velvety Robin Hood green crown, back and wing coverts and glowing violet rump. They are short-tailed and short-winged compared to Tree Swallow.
Text: On page 220 the last five words in the fourth sentence are new and from us. Since Tree Swallow has longer, more opaque wings and a longer tail, the two are easily separable when flying, far above as they are often seen.

TREE SWALLOW – On page 221 the birds have only one big

problem–they are the wrong color!! **In Life** the crown, back, wing coverts and rump of adult Tree Swallows are cobalt blue, not green. The real color is more like the fore-crown of the male Purple Martin at the bottom of page 221. **Text:** On page 220 the second sentence backs up the incorrect illustration.

BANK SWALLOW – **Text:** On page 220 note that the wings of Bank are opaque (while those of Rough-winged are translucent) and that from above there is a gray rump/brown back contrast (uniform brown in Rough-winged). Since these are primary differences it seems that if know they should have been brought up.

PURPLE MARTIN – On page 221 the flying female needs help. **In Life** they do not have ventral streaks and they do have a pale gray nuchal collar. This collar is one of the best marks (especially when dealing with Gray-breasted Martin) and should have been shared.

Because of nest site predation by Starlings the species is now rare in most of the west.

STELLER'S JAY – **Text:** On page 222 add at the end that there is also a lovely and musical whisper song. Note, too, that numerous hybrids between Steller's and Blue Jays have been spotted on the east slope of the Rockies.
Map: On page 222 add that the species is a common resident in the higher Sierra San Pedro Martir in northern Baja.

SCRUB JAY – **Text:** On page 222 the last sentence is reaching. Scrub Jays do not sound much like Steller's Jays at all on a critical level. The most common of Scrub Jay's vocal portfolio is a loud, rising 'weeek-weeek."

PINYON JAY – **Map:** On page 222 add that this species is irregularly abundant in the higher Sierra San Pedro Martir of northern Baja.

GRAY JAY – On page 225 the tail is not the right shape and lacks the correct pattern. **In Life** Gray Jays have really round, even, wedge-shaped tails. That is, the central pair of rectrices are longest and each outer pair shorter to the outermost which are shortest. Also, each feather is clearly and broadly tipped off-white.

MAGPIES – On page 225 the attempt to illustrate iridescence may mislead someone. **In Life** these birds have black tails which under particular lighting conditions gleam oily green and purple.
Text: The most usual call of both species is a husky, jay-like "wah-wah-wah-wah" in rapid series, slightly rising.

CHIHUAHUAN RAVEN – **Text**: On page 226 add that the most common call is a simple quack which sounds a lot like that of a female Green-winged Teal.

NORTHWESTERN CROW – **Map**: On page 226 it needs saying somewhere that in the southern part of the range they have so thoroughly interbred with the Common Crow that in coastal Washington and coastal mainland British Columbia most individuals may not be identified. Inland they may be called Commons and on Vancouver Island (like Clover Point) they are Northwestern. These two types of crows do not behave like distinct species should!

MOUNTAIN CHICKADEE – On page 229 the colors on the sides and back are a bit too warm. **In Life** Mountain Chickadees are cold looking and what isn't black or white is pale icy gray.
Text: The part in parentheses is new and from us.

CHESTNUT-BACKED CHICKADEE – **Map**: On page 228 the map should indicate permanent residency on the west slope of the Sierra Nevada as well as coastal California. This range expansion has taken place in the last quarter-century.

Plain Titmouse above; "Black-crested" Titmouse below

Note that southmost coastal birds lack chestnut on the sides. The Sierran population is part of the widespread northern race, and individuals are highly colored.

SIBERIAN TIT – **Text**: This species' extra-large white cheeks and long tail are two of the most prominent features and should be pointed out in any field guide.

PLAIN TITMOUSE – On page 231 both birds are too bicolored and possess two distinct features that simply are not real! **In Life** Plain Titmice are entirely medium gray, only very slightly darker above than below. They *do not have* big white eyerings and *do not have* any warm coloration on the flanks. They really are plain.

TUFTED (and Black-crested type) TITMICE do not have big white eyerings either. This is contrary to their portraits on page 231.

WRENTIT – On page 233 although the shape is pretty good, little else resembles Wrentit very closely. The bird shown is too dark brown, has a pale eyebrow, is too striped and has too wide and too yellow an iris. **In Life** individuals through most of the range are light brown-backed, gray-crowned, unmarked pale peach on the throat, and light brown-bellied. Those in the southern part of the range average grayer. If any streaks are present they are obscure and few. Real ones do not have a white eyebrow. Also the iris is white not yellow and narrower than shown (as the pupil is always dilated).
Text: The last part of the last sentence is new and good.

AMERICAN DIPPER – On page 233 the eye markings are wrong and the legs and feet are the wrong color. **In Life** dippers do not have white eyerings (though their nictating membrane is milky) and their legs and feet are pinkish horn, not bright yellow!

American Dipper

Text: On page 232 the last sentence is new and good. Add that the *call* is a rough "beet" like that of Canyon Wren and given mostly in flight.

PYGMY NUTHATCH – **Text:** On page 234 add at the end that the calls may be written as "pit - pi-dit - pi-dit" and may remind one of the "vamanos" calls of Red Crossbill.

BROWN CREEPER – **Text:** On page 234 add that the song has been written out as "trees, trees, beautiful trees." I don't know who related it but it's cute and it works.

WINTER WREN – On page 237 western ones look like the illustration but are darker above, more orangy below, especially on the throat, and not so streaky on the face and neck.
Text: The last sentence is new and from us.

BEWICK'S WREN – On page 237 the back for most individuals is too rusty. **In Life** western races (and that's about all there is anymore) are flat mouse brown above with no warm hues.
Text: The text compares its song to a House Wren when it is truly more like that of Song Sparrow.

CACTUS WREN – **Text:** Add that the usual aggressive song is machine-gun-like and might be written "wa-wa-wa-wa-wa-wa-wa-wa."

ROCK WREN – On page 239 the bird is too striped and the belly is too dull. **In Life** the whitish neck and breast are quite smooth and the belly is pale peach.
Text: Rock Wrens bob while parked and don't walk but hop.

CANYON WREN – **Text**: On page 238 add to the last sentence that the song is promptly followed by a coarse buzz or two. Also add that the call note delivered frequently while foraging is a shrill "beet" like the location note of American Dipper.

SEDGE WREN – **Text**: A very important addition is that the call note is a "chip" intermediate between that of a Yellow Warbler and that of a Lincoln's Sparrow and most unlike the voice of any other U.S. wren.
Map: No longer breeds in much of extreme Northeast shown on map.

LONG-BILLED THRASHER – On page 241 the bird is too gray and the eye color is wrong. **In Life** the tail is quite rusty (like Brown Thrasher) and the wings and back are only slightly duller. The crown is brown contrasting the gray face and sides of neck. Adults actually have orange irises and immatures have yellow. My book shows green which is not true.

BENDIRE'S THRASHER – **Map**: On page 242 note that Bendire's Thrasher is *not* a widespread resident of Baja as shown. The closely related but specifically separate Gray Thrasher is, however, and that may be the source of this mistake.

CURVE-BILLED THRASHER – On page 243 the upperparts are too gray for many birds. **In Life** the race *palmeri* is grayish brown above, the spotting below is less evident, and the iris color is yellow.
Text: The third sentence is new and from us. Dontcha wonder how many juvenile Curve-billeds have been added to lists as Bendire's?

CALIFORNIA THRASHER – On page 243 the undertail coverts are too dull and the underparts too bicolored. **In Life** the underparts are more uniform brown and the crissum is distinctly orange. This species is quite like Crissal Thrasher, more so than the pictures show.

LECONTE'S THRASHER – On page 243 the crissum should be peachy and noticeable on the otherwise colorless bird. The tail itself is black.
Text: The last sentence is so like what Peterson said in his Field Guide to Western Birds that it is amazing. Unfortunately, neither says much at all of value. LeConte's actually is a very regular singer during its breeding season (January through March), and that song is typically mimid. Add that the primary call is a "tirup" rising on the second syllable vaguely like Curve-billed Thrasher but less abrupt and more honking on second syllable.

CRISSAL THRASHER – See above what we say about California Thrasher.

RUFOUS-BACKED ROBIN – On page 245 the marks that are diagnostic are under-emphasized. **In Life** the throat is white with sharp, black streaks, the nape and upper back are gray and the back itself is, well, rufous.
Text: On page 245 because it is a valuable identification feature (behaviorally) it should be mentioned that unlike the American Robin this species is timid and a skulker (uses thick vegetation for concealment). Also add that by far the commonest call is a high buzzy "zeet."

CLAY-COLORED ROBIN – On page 245 the bird's coloration is too bright. **In Life** the upperparts are about mouse brown and the breast brownish gray and the belly becoming buffy. Also the bill should be dull yellow not bright yellow.
Text: On page 245 add somewhere that like the Rufous-backed Robin (see above) this species is timid and a skulker.

VARIED THRUSH – On page 247 there might have been a small illustration of a flying bird (maybe instead of Dusky

Thrush) to show one super mark. **In Life** Varied Thrushes flying above are easily told from similar American Robins by their shorter tails and broad, long, apricot wingstripe from the body clear through the base of the primaries.
Text: The last sentence is new and from us. Add that another call is a liquid "chup" like that of Hermit Thrush but larger.

TOWNSEND'S SOLITAIRE – On page 247 the adult really is good and the only problem is at the eye. **In Life** the eyering is broken or very narrow at the front and the lores are clear gray without black and white stripes.

BLUETHROAT – On page 247 the legs are the wrong color. **In Life** the legs and feet of this and Siberian Rubythroat are blackish.
Text: On page 246 the last three words of the last sentence are new and instructive and from us.

HERMIT THRUSH – **Text**: On page 248 add that the call note is a liquid "chup" often doubled.

SWAINSON'S THRUSH – On page 249 the back and sides are too gray for west coastal (southeast Alaska to southern California) breeders. **In Life** west coastal birds (west of Cascade-Sierra) have uniform rich brown upperparts and distinctly tan sides and flanks. Other races are olive to olive-gray above.
Text: The common call note heard from west coastal birds on breeding territory and during migration is a short, hollow, whistled "foot," and a sound which has been written "queeah" is the standard noise one hears from overhead migrants at night.

GRAY-CHEEKED THRUSH – On page 249 the eye markings and breast color are different in many individuals especially in Autumn. **In Life** most fall Gray-cheekeds have a very narrow but distinct whitish (buff in Swainson's) partial eyering bracketing the rear of the eye. The breast color beneath the arrowhead spots is creamy tan. Also the leg and foot color is pinkish horn like the other Catharas, not different as shown!

VEERY – On page 249 the eyerings are too bold for most examples and the sides and flanks too white. **In Life** Veeries have *little or no* eyering (and certainly not spectacles like the one on the left) and like western Hermits but unlike Swainson's Thrush the sides and flanks are broadly gray.

WESTERN BLUEBIRD – **Text**: On page 250 the last six words in the second-to-the-last sentence are not too helpful. **In Life** a full, lisped "thow" is its unique flightnote.

MOUNTAIN BLUEBIRD – On page 250 the job is commendable and this species really does (usually) stand with legs extended.

BLACK-CAPPED GNATCATCHER – On page 253 the bill is too small, the black cap is not quite the right shape and the feet are missing. **In Life** these birds have possibly 10 percent bigger (deeper) bills than our two (or three) regular gnatcatchers. Also the black cap should be a bit lower behind the eye and a distinct, sharp peninsula of the black cap should invade the white neck below the nape. Also this species has feet, much like other gnatcatchers.

BLACK-TAILED GNATCATCHER – On page 253 note that the race *californica* is grayer below, has different vocalizations and is likely a separate species.
Text: On page 252 it suggests that we identify females by call but, except for sonogram, there is no description of voice. The calls of both races are lower and rougher than those of Blue-gray Gnatcatcher and some are more like those of Bewick's Wren or a kitten.

KINGLETS – On page 253 all of these birds are too dull, the anterior wingbar is too evident, and the wing panel is not bright enough. **In Life** most fresh plumaged kinglets of both species are rather green above and quite yellow below. Also in both species the front wingbar is so small as to be nearly unnoticeable and the wing panel (the rectangle on the wing formed by the leading edges of the closed flight feathers) is bright chartreuse (a bit yellower in Golden).
Text: Under Ruby-crowned note that Hutton's Vireo, a serious look-alike, has a short tail and flicks its wings kinglet-like when agitated. Also add at the end that when agitated western Ruby-crowneds have a monotonous, nagging "a-a-a-a-a-a-a" very quick and slightly dropping. A quick 'chi-dit" is the standard call note, country-wide.

ARCTIC WARBLER – On page 255 that bird is much too brown for many (all) real Arctic Warblers. **In Life** at least the ones that breed in Alaska are quite pale yellow below and quite green above with white crissums. Except for the heavy bill the bird could be easily passed off as an autumn Tennessee Warbler and its song could be mistaken for that of an Orange-crowned Warbler.

BLACK-BACKED WAGTAIL – **Text:** On page 254 under White Wagtail it should have been pointed out that basic plumaged immature *M. lugens* can perhaps not be separable from *M. alba* as far as we now know. According to records in North America, the Black-backed Wagtail appears to be the more likely of the two south of Alaska though both have been identified.

GRAY WAGTAIL On page 255 a major field mark is missing (it is not mentioned in the text either), and a small, flying sketch would have been appropriate. **In Life** Gray Wags have a white or lemon *wingstripe* which is very obvious in flight and not like the wings of any North American Wagtail.

Sprague's Pipit

OLIVE TREE-PIPIT – On page 257 the back is too gray and the light eyebrow is unbroken. **In Life** these birds have obvious greenish olive hues on the back. This is the Olive, Tree-Pipit, not the Olive-Tree Pipit. Also, the pale eyebrow is actually split.

RED-THROATED PIPIT – On page 257 the face pattern is weak and the back too plain. **In Life** winter Red-throated Pipits have quite a distinctive face. The white malar mark curls up around the rear side of the dark auriculars to almost meet the posterior end of the supercillum. Also, the back stripes should be more distinctly dark and light and many (all?) individuals have two converging buffy back stripes as does the Pechora Pipit. The lower breast, belly and crissum of autumn Red-throated Pipits are white, not pink or cream as shown.

WATER PIPIT – On page 257 the "winter" plumaged bird is too dark capped, too stripy backed, too white-throated, too plain breasted and has far too distinct a face pattern and wing bars. **In Life** the crown and back are more uniform than shown, both being nearly unmarked gray (more like the "summer" bird) and have all tan throat and breast with indistinct and disorderly rows of brown streaks. The face is more expressionless with gray crown, light grayish brown cheek and indistinct tan eyebrow. As a matter of fact, treatment of this species would have been more precise if the image of the "winter" bird had been left out. Also, legs and feet of fall and winter birds can be pinkish horn, especially in Alaska and in Siberiasian races.

SPRAGUE'S PIPIT – On page 257 it appears that maybe the specimen or photo used to paint the picture was the wrong species. **In Life** Sprague's Pipits do not have a distinct white eyebrow or whisker mark, they do not have contrasty dark ear coverts, do not have the eye at the base of the bill, do not have black malar streaks, do not have bold, black streaks

down the breast and sides, do not have notably dark wing coverts. Furthermore, they *do* have a thick, short bill which is entirely pinkish except the tip of the upper mandible; the cresty forecrown extends farther out on the bill; the back feathers are the darkest on the bird and each is fully edged with pale tan or buff. **In Life** they just don't look much like this. See the Master Guide, Volume III, page 80 for photos of real-life Sprague's Pipits.
Map: Sprague's Pipits winter regularly to eastern Arizona and perhaps to parts of Southeastern California.

BLACK-CAPPED VIREO – On page 263 the male's eye is the wrong color, the spectacles are too skimpy, the back is the wrong color, the sides are too dull and the wing panel is too yellow. The female has even more problems. **In Life** male Black-capped Vireos have shining black caps, red irises and clashing, *wide* white eyrings. The back is yellow-green and the sides and flanks lemon yellow, exquisite against the immaculate white belly. The wing panel is chartreuse like a kinglet, not mustard yellow.

GRAY VIREO – On page 263 the head is too flat, the eye-ring is wrong and the tail appears relatively too short. **In Life** Gray Vireos have quite rounded heads (making the bill look smaller than in this illustration) and nice round white eye-rings. There are not black and white extensions from the eye-ring to the bill. Also these are relatively long-tailed vireos, emphasized by their short wings.
Text: The first word is new and the fourth sentence has been seriously revised by us to correct the former text.

SOLITARY VIREO – On page 263 there is one distinctive race which has been omitted. **In Life** *V. s. cassinnii,* the west coastal form, is greenish gray-capped, olive-backed, and washed with creamy yellow below. It looks more like Hutton's Vireo than either of the pictures. Of course, like most vireos these birds have pale blue or blue-gray legs and feet, not dark gray or black. The photo at the bottom of page 101, Volume III, of the Master Guide is a good picture of *V. s. cassinii* even though it is labeled *V. s. plumbeous.*

WHITE-EYED VIREO – On page 265 the facial coloration is wrong. **In Life** the lores are broadly chrome yellow including narrowly around the eye but with a smudge of dusky from the eye to the gape. Also, the eye should be bigger and set farther back on the head. The pupil should be more dilated presenting the alarmed look that this species has.

BELL'S VIREO – On page 265 there is little chance that one could identify a Bell's Vireo in the west by using this picture. The crown, back and rump are too green, the flanks and crissum are too yellow, the head is too slick, the eye markings are inaccurate, and the tail looks too short. **In Life** the western races of Bell's Vireo are basically gray above and whitish below, sometimes with a tinge of yellowish on the flanks. In all Bell's, the crown feathers are often held slightly erected giving them a defiant look and there is a wispy eyebrow (to behind the eye) and a weak under-eyering. They are *not* spectacled as shown. They are fairly long-tailed.
Text: The fifth sentence is new since we provided the above information. **Add** that this species nervously flicks its tail, too (see Gray Vireo and what the previous edition said about Gray Vireo). Imagine how many people might have counted Gray Vireo having seen a western Bell's in Arizona that was gray, was not spectacled, and that flicked its tail, with only the previous edition of this guide to go by. Imagine with even this edition . . .

HUTTON'S VIREO – On page 265 the bird is too colorless, the head is too small and the eyering too narrow. **In Life** Hutton's are olive green above, dull yellow below, have larger heads and have twice as broad an eyering. They also have thick, bluish-gray legs.
Text: On page 264 add that this species may act nervous and

flitty like Ruby-crowned Kinglet when agitated. Also add that there is a nagging 'waaa-a-a-a-a" dropping near the end that is given throughout the year.

YELLOW-THROATED VIREO – On page 265 the legs and feet are too dark. Really, they should be light blue to pale gray.
Text: On page 264 you may want to add that the song is very much like that of Solitary Vireo but wheezier.

RED-EYED VIREO – On page 267 the immature might be yellower below, the yellow-green race is too whitish below and brown above, and, of course, all the legs and feet are too dark. **In Life** immature Red-eyeds have considerable yellow on the sides and flanks. Yellow-green Vireos are often wholly yellow below (except probably at the leg insertions where they are white) and olive-green on the back. All the birds should have blue or blue-gray legs and feet. **Note**: Keep reporting U.S. sightings of Yellow-green Vireo as its taxonomic status is not entirely settled.

PHILADELPHIA VIREO – On page 267 the upper parts are much too brown, the black transocular line too distinct and the legs and feet too dark. **In Life** Philadelphia Vireos have pale gray crowns which are sharply separated from their olive-green backs. In many individuals the black line *through* the eye is obscure (in fresh juvenal plumage those dark-based feathers actually have greenish tips), but the loreal area always has a dark line. Like the other vireos, these should have blue-gray legs and feet.

WARBLING VIREO – On page 267 the crown is too slick, the eye is too small and the legs and feet are too dark. **In Life** Warbling Vireos have a gentle look to the face because the short crown feathers are usually held up and the large, dark eye has only a broad, borderless superciliary to break its position. They, too, have pale blue or blue-gray legs and feet.

BLACK-AND-WHITE WARBLER – On page 270 or 271 it might have been brought up that immature females have tan undertail coverts and lower bellies with obscure gray streaks while males have white with bold black streaks.
Map: The bird is a sparse migrant and winter visitor to California, Arizona and other western states.

SWAINSON'S WARBLER – On page 271 the underparts and eyebrow stripe are too white, the back is too colorless, and the crown lacks an obvious mark. **In Life** the underparts and broad eyebrow stripe are entirely warm tan, and the back, wings and tail are towhee brown with a faint greenish aura. The cinnamon crown is quite cresty when the bird is agitated or is singing and there is a tiny stripe onto the crown from the base of the culmen which is the same color as the eyebrow. It is like a median crown stripe was begun and then the plan was abandoned.
Text: An anthropomorphic interpretation of the song which helps to remember it is "Hide, hide, I can hide."

TENNESSEE WARBLER – On page 275 the immature is too green below and has too strong a black transocular. **In Life** fall immatures have lime backs and lemon breasts. They have a smooth, waxy look. Their faces are rather blank.

ORANGE-CROWNED WARBLER – On page 275 the "gray race" is too gray. Actually, the "eastern" and "rocky mountain" races are yellow below and green-backed with various amounts of gray on the head. Some are gray-hooded and have been mistaken for MacGillivray's.

NASHVILLE WARBLER – On page 275 there is an extra white line on the faces! **In Life** Nashvilles have clear, white, circular eyerings. That's it. There is no white line connecting the eyering to the bill and creating a spectacled look as shown.

OLIVE WARBLER – On page 275 the wing panel is the

wrong color and a very good mark in the tail is missing from both pictures and text. **In Life** there is a chartreuse panel in the closed wing formed by stacking the leading edges of the inner primaries and secondaries. Also this species has white outer tail feathers like a Townsend's Warbler.

COLIMA WARBLER – On page 277 the underparts are too white and there is an extra line on the face! **In Life** the underparts, especially the breast and throat are rather dark gray, much different than in Virginia's Warbler. As in Nashville (above), the big white eyering stands alone on the gray face and is not connected to the bill by a white stripe, forming spectacles.

CAPE MAY WARBLER – On page 279 the adult male is too green and yellow, has too short a nuchal collar, lacks a major mark on the face, and has a facial mark which does not exist. **In Life** the yellow hues are not this bright and are really more creamy, especially below the upper breast. The back is not as green but more gray-green with narrower black stripes. The yellow nuchal collar is more orangy-yellow and in profile appears to connect on the nape. Male Cape Mays have bold black transocular lines especially from the eye to the bill, which is not clear in the drawing, and they do not have big yellow eyerings.

MAGNOLIA WARBLER – On page 279 the face of the "immature female" is not like reality. **In Life** the crown and cheeks are paler and blend more into the yellow throat. Immature Magnolias do not have bold white spectacles as shown but have a narrow white ring broken before and behind the eye.

TOWNSEND'S WARBLER – On page 281 note that adult males in winter look just like they do in summer.

BLACK-THROATED BLUE WARBLER – On page 283 the

female's cheek is too light. **In Life**, although females vary a lot in plumage, the cheek or auriculars are the darkest part of the bird, sometimes almost blackish.

CHESTNUT-SIDED WARBLER – On page 285 the cheeks and throat of the "immature female" are too white. Real ones have medium gray faces and throats which helps to emphasize and isolate the bold, round, white eyring.

BAY-BREASTED WARBLER – On page 285 the immature is too dull on the front end and too uniform below. **In Life** the forecrown, chin and throat are bright yellow, greening on the nape and back and paleing yellow on the breast. Most individuals are yellow-breasted, white-bellied and cream to tan on the undertail coverts.
Text: On page 284 it might have been emphasized that the unstreaked breast (not mentioned although illustrated) is a good distinguishing character from immature Blackpoll.

BLACKPOLL WARBLER – On page 285 the immature is not bright enough. **In Life** these birds are really yellow on the face, throat and breast (even dull ones), and for unknown reasons most artists choose to paint them duller than they really are. Is this because some early artist made the mistake and all others have followed? It can't be hard to step outside some autumn morning and really look at one. Even in California!!
Text: On page 284 the parenthesized words are new and from us and are very instructive. Also the last nineteen words in that sentence may be misleading as at least a dozen other species of warblers share these characters in autumn.
Map: A few red streaks should be splashed down the California coast (as there are for Bay-breasted) since Blackpoll is a much more regular fall migrant.

PINE WARBLER – On page 287 the male's sides are too boring and the immature female is incorrect. **In Life** adult male

Pines have bold black streaks on smooth yellow sides like Prairie Warbler. Immatures have bolder and darker facial patterns than shown and a brown wash on the flanks.
Text: On page 286 the third sentence is magnificent. Is this like the problem we have with Cedar Waxwings away from cedars or Chimney Swifts up in the sky?

PRAIRIE WARBLER – On page 287 the "immature" is too white-throated, and all illustrated may be too white on the belly-undertail coverts. **In Life** the throat is whitish yellow but not sharply defined and the best way to tell them is by the face pattern which is a ghost of that of adults. Also, most immatures have some yellow feathering in the white belly-undertail coverts, and adults, especially males, may be entirely yellow below.
Text: On page 286 the first six words of sentence two could be changed slightly to clarify a big difference. Whereas Palm Warblers pump their tails, Prairies swing theirs in an unbalanced ellipse.

PALM WARBLER – On page 287 the immature female is too white below and the facial pattern is wrong. **In Life** the entire underparts are an even tan with a string of blurry brown streaks throughout. The face is lighter brown than shown and there is a long, tan eyebrow evident especially behind the eye.

MAC GILLIVRAY'S WARBLER – On page 291 the eyerings of the birds are slightly the wrong shape and the throat of the immature is the wrong color. **In Life** the eyering of MacGillivray's is unique. There are crescent-moon shaped white marks above and below the eye. That is, the white directly above and below the eye is thicker than the white nearest the front and rear of the eye near the black breaks. Also, the immature chin and throat are not gray and white streaked but are washed with definite tan.
Text: Add at the end that the call note frequently given is a low chip like that of Common Yellowthroat but not as hoarse,

and that there is a "seet" flight note rarely heard which is not as loud as that from Connecticut.

MOURNING WARBLER – On page 291 the head of the immature is pretty good though the eyering is too dull and the throat color is variable. **In Life** the eyering is like the adult female MacGillivray's shown above, and the throat is whitish tan often washed with lemon yellow.
Text: Add at the end that the usual call note is a brief "yak" like that from Bewick's Wren but not as blurry, and that there is a weak "seet" flight note like that from MacGillivray's Warbler.

CONNECTICUT WARBLER – On page 290 the hood of the immature is too gray and the eyering too weak. The legs of all three birds are too dull. **In Life** fall immature Connecticuts have almost uniform olive-brown upperparts including the nape and crown. The cheeks and throat are brown, not gray, and the creamy eyering is complete and very obvious.
Text: Since it is a good differentiation it should be said that this species *walks* (on the ground and on branches) while MacGillivray's and Mournings *hop.* Add at the end that there is a rough "seet" flightnote like that from Yellow Warbler but louder.

HOODED WARBLER – **Text:** On page 292 add that the call note is a sharp "pink" like that from a west coastal Brown Towhee.

WILSON'S WARBLER – On page 293 the picture of the female represents only one of three races. **In Life** adult females of *W. p. pusilla* and *W. p. chryseola* (the eastern and western forms) have black caps like the males. They are a flat black, not shining like males', but they are definite.
Text: On page 292 add that the call note is very much like a single note from Winter Wren.

Bobolink

CANADA WARBLER – On page 293 the undertail coverts are the wrong color. **In Life** those feathers are bright white sharply contrasting the bright yellow belly.

RED-FACED WARBLER – On page 293 the tail is too short and appears too rigid. **In Life** this species has an unusually long, floppy tail (compared to most *temperate* wood warblers).

PAINTED REDSTART – On page 293 (or 292) since *juvenal* plumage is different and since that is a plumage that many birders see, it should have been mentioned if not pictured. **In Life** juvenal plumage which is worn for a couple of weeks after fledging is rather like the adult but the red breast and much of the white belly are replaced by charcoal gray.

We will not be dealing with pages 294 and 295 as some of the species could easily become extinct by the time we would finish. Briefly, however, some of these pictures are better than those in the text, for instance, Connecticut, Canada, Chestnut-sided, Magnolia and Prairie.

BOBOLINK – On page 297 the fall bird is too brown and the back is wrong. **In Life** autumn Bobolinks are bright yellow on the face, breast and sides and have converging buffy stripes on the back (where the summer male has white ones).
Text: Add that a dull "ink" flight note is unique.

EASTERN MEADOWLARK – On page 297 (or 296) it should have been told that southwestern Easterns have one more white tail feather on each side than do Westerns or eastern Easterns and can be identified by it when landing. For that form it appears to be a white tail with a rectangular dark center rather than a dark tail with white margins.
Map: This species breeds west to eastern Colorado, southwestern South Dakota and western Nebraska.

RUSTY BLACKBIRD – **Text:** On page 298 words 15–19 in the third sentence are new and pertinent. Also see the last sentence under Brewer's Blackbird which is relevant.

BREWER'S BLACKBIRD – **Text:** On page 298 the first word of the last sentence is new and of much value.

BOAT-TAILED GRACKLE – On page 301 not only are their legs positioned in a highly unlikely manner but the crowns are too sleek and the tails relatively too long. **In Life** Boat-taileds are slightly cresty compared to Great-taileds and their tails are perhaps 25 percent shorter. Also all the birds edging the Gulf of Mexico and on peninsular Florida have brown eyes.

GREAT-TAILED GRACKLE – On page 301 the attempt to illustrate iridescence has gone too far. **In Life** the birds are not all purple but actually look a lot more like the illustration of male Boat-tailed Grackle (which they were in the last edition).

BROWN-HEADED COWBIRDS – **Text:** On page 300 the second-to-the-last sentence is a bit misleading. Actually the young are all light tan and buffy, are distinctly mottled above and striped below, and look more like carpodacus finches than icterids.

BRONZED COWBIRD – On page 301 the female illustrated is intermediate in darkness between the Arizona and Texas specimens which are quite different from each other.

ORCHARD ORIOLE – **Text:** On page 302 the last sentence is new, from us, and important for identification. Add that one English translation of the song that fits in Alabama is "First ya say ah can, then ya say ah cain't" (thanks, Harriett). Orchards at Big Bend on the western side of the range say it a little differently.

HOODED ORIOLE – On page 305 a plumage which has caused some I.D. problems is not shown. **In Life** all males in fresh plumage (early winter) which are otherwise like the adult male shown have buffy tan backs with black scales and have been called Streak-backed Orioles.
Text: The last sentence, from us, is new and good.

ALTAMIRA ORIOLE – **Text**: On page 304 the first sentence is misleading and way out of date. The species is actually a fairly common resident in suitable habitat all along the lower Rio Grande from Boca Chica to San Ygnacio. They are especially evident at Santa Ana National Wildlife Refuge and Bentsen and Falcon Texas State Parks where they are fed by Winnebago pilgrims. Also the third sentence is misleading as it is not easy to tell which bird of a breeding pair is which sex. They are virtually monotypic.

SCARLET TANAGER – On page 307 another plumage might have been shown (like instead of the "Fall"). **In Life** many immatures wearing their first set of wing feathers have whitish yellow tips on median and greater coverts forming distinct wingbars. This could lead to an identification problem with Western Tanager.

SUMMER TANAGER – On page 307 the female head has a few surplus marks. **In Life** female Summer Tanagers do not have white eyerings, do not have dark auriculars, and do not have black lores to above the eye as shown.
Text: On page 306 it should be said that often, especially in late autumn, the bills of Summer Tanagers may be blackish.

NORTHERN CARDINAL – **Text**: On page 308 add at the end that the most common vocalization is a Vermivora like "tik," quiet, high and metallic.

ROSE-BREASTED GROSBEAK – On page 311 the female is overly streaked for most individuals. **In Life** there is usually a necklace of fine, more discreet streaks and a subtle row or two down the sides to the flanks.

BLACK-HEADED GROSBEAK – **Text**: On page 310 add at the end that the call note is not as sharp as that of Rose-breasted Grosbeak and is more a flat "pic" similar to Downy Woodpecker's.

EVENING GROSBEAK – **Text**: The last part of the last sentence does not completely describe voices of these birds. The primary call of Sierran birds, most often given in flight, is a high, clear, whistled "thew." The call of New England birds sounds the same.

BLUE GROSBEAK – On page 311 the female is a bit dull and immature birds (all in female plumage) are even brighter. **In Life** female plumaged birds are rich, orangy buff on the face and underparts and are unstreaked below.
Text: On page 310 add at the end that the most common vocalization is a sharp, metallic "pink."

LAZULI BUNTING – On page 310 the female is too dull on the back and breast and has a mark that real birds lack. **In Life** female (and especially immature) Lazulis have brown backs (like the crown) and peach-colored breasts. They do not have a white eyebrow as shown.

VARIED BUNTING – **Map**: On page 312 add that this species has an isolated resident population in the Cape region of Baja.

PAINTED BUNTING – On page 313 an important plumage is missing. **In Life**, juveniles into the first autumn are gray-brown with little or no green or yellow feathering. They have noticeable eyerings and pinkish-gray bills and comprise a large fraction of the whole population at that time.
Text: On page 312 add at the end that the common call note

is similar to that of Audubon's (not Myrtle) Yellow-rumped Warbler and is a short, flat "spit."

BRAMBLING – On page 315 all these birds are *way* too dull. **In Life** Bramblings have *orange* breasts, wing coverts and edges to the tertials. Winter birds have blue-gray collars and faces, corn yellow bills and a pale rectangle on the nape bordered by darker stripes.

PURPLE FINCH – On page 317 the female has the wrong undertail coverts and, for western birds, too colorless a back. **In Life** Purple Finches have unmarked white undertail coverts while Cassin's have streaked. Also, western Purples, especially in fresh plumage and good light, have olive green hues on the nape, back and wing coverts.
Text: On page 316 I have whited-out the first four words in the second-to-the-last sentence and replaced them with the contradictory "a dull, unmusical tink."

CASSIN'S FINCH – On page 317 the breast, malar and rump of the male are too red, the nape and back are too dark. The female's back is too dark, too, and her bill is too bulbous. **In Life** the breast, malar and rump are cold pink, leaving the shiny red cap by far the brightest part of the bird. Cassin's Finches are frosty looking birds and the tan nape and back stripes are separated by broad, white ones. The females, too, should have wider and whiter back stripes and smaller, paler tan back stripes. Also the culmen and gonys (in profile, the edges of the bill) are straight to a sharp point (like Pine Siskin) while Purple Finch has a curved culmen giving its whole face a different look.
Map: On page 316 add that it is resident in the higher Sierra San Pedro Martir in northern Baja. Also, the winter range on mainland Mexico is not nearly this extensive or deep.

HOUSE FINCH – **Text**: On page 316 add that a significant percentage of males (in some populations, all the males) suffer from diet deficiency and normal red feathering is replaced by yellow or orange. Add at the end that the full song reminds some of typing an entire line and throwing the carriage at the end. (Thanks, Florence.)

ROSY FINCH – On page 319 none of these birds should have eyerings. **In Life** male brown-capped Rosy's have unpatterned faces, and females are dark brown not dark gray.

REDPOLLS – On page 319 pure Hoaries have very short, almost round pyrrhuloxia-like bills compared to Commons' which are long and more siskin-like. There are many intermediates. Though scientifically unresolved there is little doubt that these are two forms of the same species.

PINE SISKIN – On page 321 the bills of all three birds are too needly and warbler-like. **In Life** siskins have classic conical bills with straight culmen and gonys that are deep based and very sharp, much like that of the perched European Goldfinch at the bottom of the page.

AMERICAN GOLDFINCH – **Text**: On page 320 the italicized words in the second-to-the-last sentence sound to some like "po-ta-to-chip" which is easier to remember since the bird flies with a dip. (Come on, Kenn!)

LESSER GOLDFINCH – On page 321 the white spot at the base of the primaries is also present on adult females and is a useful feature.

LAWRENCE'S GOLDFINCH – **Text**: The last sentence is new, from us, and once these notes are learned one would never miss the species if some were around.

DICKCISSEL – On page 323 the birds' legs are too short. **In Life** these guys have exceptionally long tarsii for passerines and often stand tall on them.

Map: Not enough Dickcissels winter on the Atlantic coast (especially north) to warrant the blue stripe.

WHITE-COLLARED SEEDEATER – On page 323 the males shown are like those in southern Mexico. Actually, those in northeast Mexico and south Texas have buffy tan underparts, brown backs and gray crowns.

GREEN-TAILED TOWHEE – On page 325 the heads of these birds, especially the adult, are too slick. **In Life,** though they sometimes look like this, most often the short crown feathers are erected, emphasizing the rustiness and giving them a pompous look.

RUFOUS-SIDED TOWHEE – **Text:** On page 325 the parenthesized words are new and from us and we are happy that the voice of our towhees may now be included in the Birds of North America.

BROWN TOWHEE – On page 325 a couple of field marks are missing. **In Life** both forms have obvious orange undertail coverts. Also the "Rocky Mt. race" has a black splotch in the center of the breast.
Text: While Pacific coastal ones call a high, piano-like "pink," those in the Chisos Mountains of west Texas call a breezy "heer" rather like a sapsucker, and southeast Arizona birds have intermediate calls.

GRASSHOPPER SPARROW – On page 329 a freshly molted autumn bird (immature especially) should be shown, as they can be very buffy orange and then may get called LeConte's. In that plumage note the gray eyebrow, yellow-orange at the very front for Grasshopper, and an *all* orange eyebrow for LeConte's. Also, Grasshopper Sparrows have two distinct converging tan or white stripes on the back like those of autumn Bobolink (not shown on that species either).
Map: On page 328 note that this species does not winter

throughout Baja. It is at best rare and only in the southern portion at that season. It no doubt breeds in the extreme northern part of the peninsula.

BAIRD'S SPARROW – On page 329 the birds are too dull. **In Life** Baird's are bright, orangy, buffy, ruddy and tan all over the upperparts.

LARK BUNTING – **Map:** On page 332 extend the blue line at least half-way down the Baja Peninsula including the Pacific slope.

JUNCOS – On page 335 the heads of "pink-sided" and "gray-headed" types are much too dark and should be pale gray.

RUFOUS-WINGED SPARROW – On page 337 the adult is too gray below. Actually they are white.

CASSIN'S SPARROW – On page 337 the plate for Cassin's and Botteri's is good for those species in fresh plumage (November-December), but unfortunately that is not when most birders see them. They are both rainy season breeders in the Southwest and are most often found by their singing in July and August. By this time natural abrasion and wear have caused the birds to appear much less patterned. Cassin's are generally grayer than Botteri's in Arizona (south Texas Botteri's are much grayer than western ones) and lack the rusty edges to their wing coverts. They also have pale whitish tips to the outer retrices and streaks on the flanks which are useful in separation from Botteri's.

BOTTERI'S SPARROW – On page 337 the back pattern, though correct, needs explanation (see above under Cassin's Sparrow). Note also that Texas Botteri's average much grayer than Arizona ones.
Text: Change the wording on page 336 to read that some

Botteri's often deliver full songs while in low flutter-flight and that there are often more than four sputtering notes before speeding into a trill.

CLAY-COLORED SPARROW – On page 339 the immature is too dull. **In Life** they are pinkish buff on the breast and sides and have a contrasty broad gray nuchal colllar.
Text: Though adequately illustrated it should be emphasized in print that the thin, dark, transocular line does not go forward from the eye to the bill (as it does in basic plumaged Chipping Sparrow) and that the lores of Clay-coloreds are pale, giving them a unique face.

BREWER'S SPARROW – **Map**: Correct this map to show that the species winters throughout Baja Sur but not Baja Norte or, in numbers, in southern California.

BLACK-CHINNED SPARROW – On page 339 it must be the printing but these birds appear dark, purplish gray. **In Life** they are pale gray like the breast of the nearest White-throated Sparrow on page 327. Also the "im" is more like an adult female. Immatures are like respective adults, juveniles are blurrily streaked, and the winter male lacks the black chin.
Map: Correct this map to show that the species winters in the Cape region of Baja but not north of there on the peninsula. They do winter sparingly in southern Arizona and northern Sonora.

GOLDEN-CROWNED SPARROW – On page 341 the bird labeled "im." is not necessarily that. Unlike White-crowned Sparrows which have immature and adult crown patterns, Golden-crowneds have basic and alternate. That is, a bird with a full "adult" crown departing in April will return in early October as an "immature" or "second winter."
Text: On page 340 the reorganization of the last sentence and especially the italicized words are new and from us.

FOX SPARROW – On page 343 there are only two representatives of this highly diverse species. One more image would be most appropriate. **In Life** birds that nest in the U.S. Rockies and Sierra Nevada are unmarked pale gray on the face, crown, nape and back, have dull brown wings and rusty brown rumps and tails. The dark brown markings below are neater than those of other races. Sierran birds' call note is a metallic "pink" very much like that from coastal Brown Towhees while winter birds from Canada have a louder, flat "chich" like a big Lincoln Sparrow's.

LINCOLN SPARROW – On page 343 the supercilium is the wrong color. It may seem like a small point but this mark gives the face a special look by which the species may be identified. Also, the crown is too sleek for those most often seen. **In Life** that eyebrow mark is even, medium gray, *not white* and usually appears broader than shown. Lincoln's when agitated raise their short crown feathers and look bushy-headed. Being pished or squeaked out invariably agitates them.

SWAMP SPARROW – **Text:** On page 342 add at the end that the call note is very much like the single call of Black or Eastern Phoebe.
Map: Oops! Swamp Sparrows are rare to uncommon (locally fairly common, like twenty in one small area) in winter along the west coast from northern Washington to southern California as well as at damp spots inland and including southern Nevada and Arizona.

SONG SPARROW – On page 343 the "brown race" looks just like the "gray race." **In Life** there are so many geographic varieties of Song Sparrow (which span the arena from pallid grayish-white with hardly any streaking to blackish and rusty ones spotted like Fox Sparrows) that it seems odd that two at more distant ends of the cline were not selected for illustration.

Text: On page 342 remember that all three *Melospiza* sparrows pump their tails in flight and that the common call note for Song Sparrow, which is distinctive, might be put down as a hollow "shimp."

McCOWN'S LONGSPUR – On page 345 the male is too white and has a subtly mistaken facial pattern, and the bill is too small. **In Life** the eyebrow, throat and underparts are more ashy gray, and most birds lack a dark post ocular stripe. Also, the chestnut median coverts show more extensively, and the bill which is larger than other longspurs' is pinkish in females and winter males.

CHESTNUT-COLLARED LONGSPUR – On page 345 the proportions are misleading, the bills are the wrong color, and the alternate plumaged bird has too pale a face. **In Life** these birds look smaller-headed than the pictures imply; the bills are gray, not yellow; and more black intrudes to the eye from the crown and post ocular.
Text: On page 344 add a simple sentence at the end: "Yes it does!" Chestnut-collareds often give a typical longspur rattle especially when scared into flight. Also add that some winter birds have a white wing patch like Smith's Longspur!

LAPLAND LONGSPUR – On page 345 the female looks more like a juvenile with its colorless body, weak face pattern and streaked breast. **In Life** all birds by late fall have some rust on the back of the neck, greater wing coverts and tertial edges; have sharp face patterns; and lack breast streaking. It is basic-plumaged Chestnut-collared Longspurs that are typically streaked across the breast.
Text: On page 344 the last four words are new and from us.

SMITH'S LONGSPUR – **Text**: On page 345 the words in parentheses are new from us and can save problems.

McKAY'S BUNTING – On page 345 the winter female looks just like a Snow Bunting and not so much like McKay's.

RUSTIC BUNTING – Where is it? A very regular visitor to the outer Aleutians with records for southwestern British Columbia and northern California. There were over 100 records at Attu in a two-week period. This is one of the more common rare-strays and deserves a niche in the book somewhere.

INDEX